Political Dimensions of the American Macroeconomy

Political Dimensions of the American Macroeconomy

Second Edition

Gerald T. Fox

BEP BUSINESS EXPERT PRESS

First published in 2020 by
Business Expert Press, LLC
222 East 46th Street, New York, NY 10017
www.businessexpertpress.com

ISBN-13: 978-1-94897-635-0 (paperback)
ISBN-13: 978-1-94897-636-7 (e-book)

Business Expert Press Economics and Public Policy Collection

Collection ISSN: 2163-761x (print)
Collection ISSN: 2163-7628 (electronic)

Cover image licensed by Ingram Image, StockPhotoSecrets.com
Cover and interior design by S4Carlisle Publishing Services Private Ltd., Chennai, India

First edition: 2015
Second edition: 2020

10 9 8 7 6 5 4 3 2 1

Printed in the United States of America.

Abstract

Political macroeconomy refers to the interconnection between macroeconomic politics and macroeconomic performance. The expectational Phillips curve may be used to examine the economic aspects of this interrelation. *Macroeconomic politics* relates to voter behavior, presidential reelection ambition, partisan economic priorities, and special interests. These factors impact the fiscal and monetary policy actions of the president, Congress, and central bank.

According to the electoral effect, presidents attempt to boost the economy before an election to increase reelection votes. According to the partisan effect, conservative presidencies are relatively inflation averse, while liberal administrations are relatively unemployment averse. The evidence, however, suggests that the electoral and partisan effects occurred idiosyncratically in the U.S. economy during 1961–2016.

The economy also affects presidential approval, Congressional elections, consumer sentiment, voter participation, and macropartisanship. An international dimension of the political macroeconomy is the issue of free trade versus protectionism and the perspectives of economic liberalism, neomercantilism, and structuralism.

Keywords

classical macroeconomic perspective; congressional vote; electoral cycle; expectations-augmented Phillips curve; fiscal policy; inflation; Keynesianism; median voter model; monetary policy; partisan cycle; political business cycle; presidential approval; presidential vote; unemployment

Contents

Acknowledgments

This book is based on research and study over the last two decades. I wish to thank the many anonymous referees who reviewed my research and provided valuable suggestions. I would like to thank High Point University for allowing me the time to complete this book. I wish to express appreciation to individuals affiliated with Business Expert Press who provided encouragement, suggestions, and motivation; they include Jeff Edwards, Phillip Romero, Scott Isenberg, and Chithra Amaravel. I am grateful to the team at S4 Carlisle in overseeing the production of this book. Moreover, I wish to thank my dear wife Mayumi for her patience and support while I undertook this project.

CHAPTER 1

The Political Macroeconomy

Macroeconomics and National Politics

The relation between national politics and the macroeconomy is always a timely and relevant subject. Public perceptions of the president and the Congress are affected by whether the economy is strong or weak. Citizens reward political incumbents with increased reelection votes if a strong economy occurs. Citizens punish incumbents with reduced votes if a weak economy occurs. Politicians consequently promote policies they think will attain strong economic performance to increase their likelihood of reelection.

This book addresses some concepts, issues, and evidence on the interrelation between American national politics and the U.S. macroeconomy. Electoral, partisan, and other political pressures affect the macroeconomic policy and the state of the economy. The state of the economy, in turn, affects election outcomes, public sentiment, partisan pressures, and other political considerations.

An overview of the main concepts of the political macroeconomy may be expressed using a triangle flow diagram. The Political macroeconomy consists of three elements: (1) macroeconomic politics, (2) macroeconomic policy, and (3) macroeconomic outcomes. Figure 1.1 shows the triangle flow diagram.

Electoral and partisan politics, the policy preferences among policymakers, and the interactions among the macroeconomic policymakers determine macroeconomic policies. The three main macroeconomic policymakers are the president, the Congress, and the central bank (i.e., Federal Reserve or Fed). Macroeconomic policies, in the form of fiscal and monetary measures, affect macroeconomic outcomes such as gross domestic product (GDP), unemployment, inflation, and interest rates.

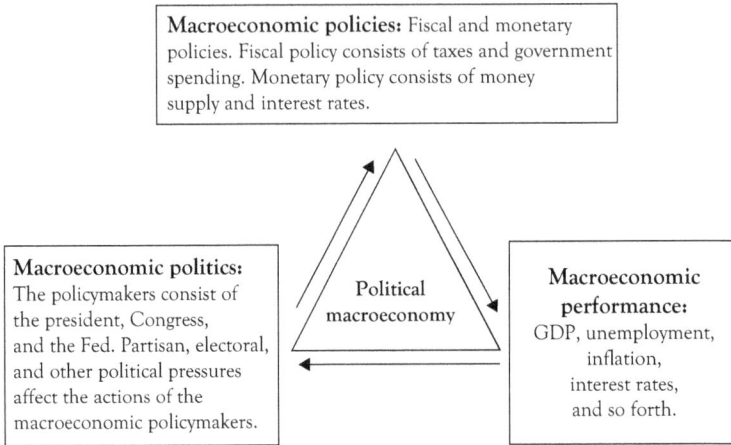

Figure 1.1 Triangle flow of the political macroeconomy

The condition of the economy then impacts public opinion and voter behavior regarding elected politicians.

Macroeconomic Politics Influence Macroeconomic Policies

Macroeconomic politics are national political pressures that influence the macroeconomic policy actions of elected politicians and the central bank. Two main categories of political pressure impact the macroeconomic policy actions of the president and the Congress, and to some degree the central bank.

The two main categories of political pressure are electoral politics and partisan politics. Special interests can also affect macroeconomic policy decisions. The impact of special interests on macroeconomic policy, however, partially overlaps with partisan influence. This occurs because special interest groups tend to be aligned with political parties. Labor interests, for example, tend to align with the political left, while business interests tend to align with the political right.

- *Electoral macroeconomic politics*: The public exerts political pressure on the president and the Congress to adopt macroeconomic policies that accomplish the economic interests of voters. Electoral influence occurs through the voting process and public opinion.

Some factors that weigh on public opinion and voting behavior are the state of the economy, media activity, and the views of opinion leaders in society. The president and congressional legislators typically seek reelection. Consequently, elected officials consider the macroeconomic preferences of voters in determining the macroeconomic policy to improve reelection prospects.

- *Partisan macroeconomic politics*: Political parties exert pressure on member politicians to adhere to partisan economic platforms. To receive political party endorsements, politicians tend to support the preferred macroeconomic policies of their political parties. The partisan influence theory asserts that the political right (Republican party) tends to be relatively inflation averse in its macroeconomic policy preference, while the political left (Democratic party) tends to be relatively unemployment averse.

Electoral and partisan pressures affect the macroeconomic policy actions of the macroeconomic policymakers. Macroeconomic policies consist of fiscal measures and monetary measures. The fiscal policy mainly consists of the influence of taxes and government spending on macroeconomic outcomes. The fiscal policy occurs through the government budgetary process involving the political interaction between the Congress and the president. This interaction occurs in the context of the macroeconomic policy agendas of the conservative and liberal political parties. The president and the Congress consider voter economic attitudes and partisan macroeconomic platforms when implementing fiscal policy.

Monetary policy occurs through the actions of the Fed. The Fed chairman and the Federal Open Market Committee of the Fed are the main monetary policymakers. Monetary policy is the influence of money supply and interest rates on the macroeconomy. A simplifying assumption often made in political macroeconomic analysis is that monetary policy tends to coincide with the macroeconomic preference of the president. The realism of this assumption is addressed in Chapter 9.

Two important political influences affect monetary policy as administered by the central bank. They are the presidential appointment of the Fed chairperson and periodic congressional hearings that involve testimony by the Fed chairperson. Additionally, the monetary policy decisions by the Fed are susceptible to political pressure from financial special interests, the media, opinion leaders, and public opinion.

Macroeconomic Policies Impact Macroeconomic Performance

Chapter 2 discusses the main macroeconomic indicators, including GDP, inflation, unemployment, interest rates, and the business cycle. Understanding the main macroeconomic measurements establishes a foundation for consideration of politico-macroeconomic effects.

The business cycle is the up-and-down pattern of macroeconomic performance over time. An economic expansion or boom denotes a growing economy as measured by rising real GDP (RGDP) and declining unemployment. A recession in the business cycle denotes a declining economy as measured by decreasing RGDP and worsening unemployment. The performance of inflation during the up-phase versus the down-phase of the business cycle depends on the underlying macroeconomic supply and demand factors.

Chapter 3 examines the macroeconomic supply and demand forces that determine inflation, unemployment, and real economic growth in the short run and in the long run. The framework we will use is the expectations-augmented Phillips curve model. This model explains the interconnection between inflation and unemployment. The empirical relation of Okun's law is also examined. Okun's law expresses the empirical connection between GDP and unemployment. The three indicators of GDP, unemployment, and inflation are important considerations for political macroeconomic analysis because these variables affect voter opinions as well as presidential and congressional election outcomes. These three economic indicators are also important factors for the preferred macroeconomic agendas of the left and right political parties.

Through legislation such as the *Employment Act of 1946* and the *Full Employment and Balanced Growth Act*, the federal government has the responsibility to promote strong macroeconomic performance. Three major measures of a strong economy are high RGDP growth, low unemployment, and low stable inflation.

Chapter 4 examines macroeconomic policy, also called stabilization policy. The macroeconomic policy affects macroeconomic outcomes, such as inflation, unemployment, economic growth, and the pattern of the business cycle. The macroeconomic policy may be expansionary or contractionary. An expansionary policy seeks to attain high RGDP and low unemployment. These two macroeconomic objectives generally co-incide with each other. High economic growth tends to occur alongside low or declining unemployment as employers hire more workers to produce more goods and services.

A short-run macroeconomic trade-off, however, sometimes occurs regarding inflation. In some circumstances, the goals of high economic growth and low unemployment conflict with the other objective of low inflation. The simultaneous attainment of low inflation along with high economic growth and low unemployment is not always possible. The two goals of low unemployment and high economic growth may come at the long-run economic cost of greater inflation. For example, during the Kennedy–Johnson presidencies of the 1960s, an expansionary macroeconomic policy led to a decrease in unemployment from 6.7 to 3.6 percent, while inflation rose from 1.1 to 4.2 percent.

In contrast to an expansionary policy, the main goal of a contractionary policy is to reduce inflation. This objective, however, may occur at the short-run cost of declining real economic growth and worsening unemployment, possibly even a recession. Policymakers do not generally seek higher unemployment. In some instances, however, higher unemployment is unavoidable to bring down inflation. For example, in the early 1980s, during the first term of Ronald Reagan, the Fed sought to curb high inflation that was inherited from the oil shocks of the 1970s. Through a contractionary macroeconomic policy, inflation fell from around 10 percent in 1981 to about 3 percent in 1983. This, however, came at the cost of a severe recession and a rise in unemployment from approximately 7½ percent to more than 9½ percent.

Macroeconomic Performance Impacts Macroeconomic Politics

The condition of the economy affects various measures of public opinion and voter behavior:

- Presidential election outcomes
- Congressional election outcomes

- Presidential job approval
- Voter participation rates
- Macropartisanship
- Societal happiness index
- Consumer sentiment

These indicators of voter sentiment and behavior are discussed in Chapter 10. For example, the public holds the president accountable for the condition of the economy through the democratic process of voting and opinion polls. The conventional theory (*responsibility hypothesis*) asserts that a strong economy tends to boost presidential approval, which improves the likelihood that the incumbent or the candidate from the incumbent political party will win reelection to the presidency. The incumbent political party, or the in-party, is the party that controls the White House prior to a presidential election. The opposition political party, or the out-party, is the party that is not in control of the White House. If a Democratic president is in the White House preceding an election, then the Democratic Party is the in-party. If a Republican is in the White House prior to an election, then the Republican Party is the in-party.

The responsibility hypothesis asserts that a weak economy lessens the prospect that the in-party will gain reelection to the White House. Citizens are inclined to penalize the in-party with low reelection votes if a sluggish economy occurs. The in-party consequently has a strong incentive to establish policies that achieve strong economic performance to improve reelection chances.

Intersection between Macroeconomic Performance and Macroeconomic Politics

The main characteristics of the political macroeconomy may be shown using a Venn diagram. Figure 1.2 shows the union and intersection of the political and economic spheres of the political macroeconomy.

Macroeconomic policy occurs at the intersection between the political and macroeconomic spheres of the political macroeconomy. Macroeconomic politics—in the form of electoral and partisan pressures—impact the macroeconomic policy decisions of the president, the Congress, and

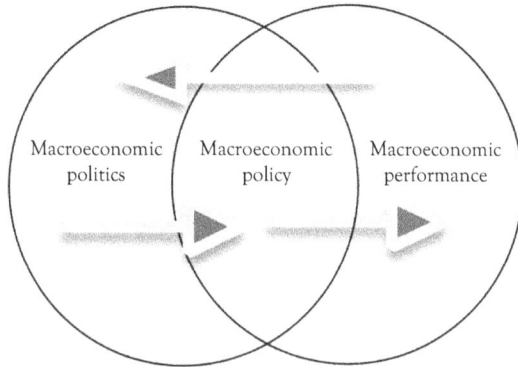

Figure 1.2 Intersection and union of the two spheres of the political macroeconomy

the Fed. Macroeconomic policies subsequently affect macroeconomic events such as GDP, unemployment, and inflation, and the pattern of the business cycle.

The macroeconomic policy may be expansionary or contractionary, based on whether the main goal of the policymakers (as influenced by partisan and electoral pressures) is to reduce unemployment or fight inflation. The level of macroeconomic performance then impacts voter attitudes, election results, and partisan economic priorities, which affects the next round of macroeconomic policy decisions by the policymakers.

Political Macroeconomy of Peace and Prosperity versus Conflict and Poverty

Another type of politico-macroeconomic effect is the relation between the economic conditions of a nation-state and its political stability. Although not an absolute generalization for all circumstances, the greater the economic prosperity of a country, the stronger the probability of political stability. Moreover, international economic prosperity among nations increases the likelihood for peaceful relations among those countries.

For example, the economic development and international trade and financial flows among western industrialized countries in the post–World War II era played a major role in the relatively peaceful relations among those nations. Countries that conduct substantial international commerce with one another are less prone to go to war against one another.

This is because the destructiveness of war disrupts the profitable flow of economic activity among nations.

Besides the link between economic prosperity and political peace and stability, a reverse causation also occurs. Economic crises, severe income inequity, and poverty tend to worsen political discontentment and strife. Economic plight is also a contributing factor to terrorism and war. A classic example was the economic collapse and hyperinflation of Germany in the aftermath of World War I. In consequence of the 1919 Treaty of Versailles and the 1921 London Ultimatum, Germany was economically penalized for starting World War I. War reparations and other stringent measures were placed on Germany as a retribution.

To manage the heavy war debt, Germany monetized much of its financial obligations. This action of excessive printing of money (monetization) to pay international war debt caused hyperinflation and economic breakdown in Germany in the early 1920s. Additionally, the subsequent worldwide Great Depression of the early 1930s compounded Germany's economic turmoil.

This economic catastrophe fueled a political climate of fascist extremism in Germany and elsewhere in the world (e.g., Italy, Japan). Hitler was able to seize political and military power in Germany because of this unstable economic and political environment. This series of economic and political crises led to the Nazi war machine and the outbreak of World War II in Europe.

Economic prosperity tends to promote political stability and peace, while poverty and economic collapse often breed social dissatisfaction and even war. Table 1.1 summarizes the interconnection between the state of the economy and political stability.

Table 1.1 Peace and prosperity versus war and poverty

Economic condition	Political consequence	Politico-macroeconomic outcome
Economic prosperity	Political stability and tranquility	Peace and prosperity
Economic breakdown	Political instability and discontent	Social conflict and poverty

The Classical View versus Keynesianism

The classical view versus Keynesianism are the two main perspectives on the role of government versus market forces in the economy. The subsequent chapters examine some implications of these two opposing perspectives regarding political ideology, macroeconomic policy and performance, political party economic preferences, and voter behavior. The two perspectives of classicism versus Keynesianism tend to be loosely aligned with the two political ideologies of the political right versus the political left.

The classical view asserts that market forces are relatively stable, efficient, and flexible. This perspective fears that government intervention in the economy often adversely distorts prices, hinders production, and causes inefficiency. This viewpoint maintains that market forces normally yield win-win or positive-sum results for buyers and sellers, including the labor and business sectors of the economy. Any adverse results from market forces that may arise, according to the classical view, are often mild and short-lived. Flexible prices and business competition in the market system will normally cure economic inefficiencies, such as a recession.

The classical perspective argues that government intervention in the economy is frequently harmful, even if well-intentioned. Government economic activism often creates unforeseen and adverse economic consequences, according to the classical view. This perspective maintains that government is usually not sufficiently well-informed to recognize and implement what is best for economic society. Even if the government possesses altruistic economic motives, the policy actions that take place often create harmful unintended consequences, such as high prices, less economic innovation, and lower economic growth.

The classical view argues that the state is often less effective than decentralized market forces in determining the economic outcomes that are best for society. The flexibility of decentralized market forces is more efficient and beneficial than government controls, regulation, and government production of goods and services.

The concept of government failure refers to the negative consequences of activist government policies on the economy. For example, the state could mistakenly or shortsightedly adopt policies that overstimulate the macroeconomy in an attempt to increase economic growth and reduce unemployment. However, a negative result of higher inflation could occur with no lasting benefit on economic growth. Another example is governmental controls that could end up overregulating, overtaxing, or otherwise over-constraining the economy in various ways, which could hinder economic growth.

The classical view states that the government's role in the economy should be relatively minor. This perspective prescribes low taxes, low government spending, and minimal government regulation of the business, labor, financial, and consumer sectors. Citizens with a classical *laissez-faire* economic outlook tend to identify with the political ideology of the conservative right. This outlook generally aligns politically with the Republican Party and other conservative political perspectives, such as libertarianism.

In contrast to the classical view, the other main macroeconomic perspective is Keynesianism. This perspective is named after John Maynard Keynes, the noted 20th century British economist. Keynes advocated an activist fiscal policy to address the Great Depression of the 1930s. The New Deal economic programs to combat the Great Depression in the United States were an example of Keynesian government stimulus. Keynesianism asserts that government intervention in the macroeconomy is sometimes necessary to resolve inefficiencies, imperfections, and rigidities in market forces. The concept of market failure denotes the detrimental side effects of market forces.

Keynesianism maintains that market forces sometimes become unstable, inflexible, and inefficient. The Keynesian view states that market forces sometimes generate market failures, especially in the labor and financial markets. Market failures arise from economic rigidities, bottlenecks, uncertainty, speculation, and excessive economic risk aversion to entrepreneurship and innovation. These potential market deficiencies generate harmful macroeconomic consequences, including the episodic occurrence of severe recessions. The Great Depression of the 1930s is the usual example of a major market failure, according to Keynesianism. In contrast to Keynesianism, many classicists (and monetarists) argue that mismanagement of monetary policy by the Fed (rather than market failure) was a major reason for the Great Depression.

Keynesianism asserts that government has a duty to intervene in the economy through macroeconomic policies to resolve recessions that otherwise could end up being long and severe. The Keynesian view prescribes expansionary macroeconomic policies to boost macroeconomic demand, also called aggregate demand. Keynesian macroeconomic stimulus seeks to create jobs and raise GDP through government intervention.

Higher government spending, lower taxes, and lower interest rates are standard Keynesian techniques aimed at alleviating weak economic performance. Individuals with a Keynesian macroeconomic outlook tend to identify with the political left ideology and the Democratic party in the United States.

The conservative and liberal political parties tend to have differing macroeconomic priorities. Chapter 7 discusses this subject and the related topic of liberal and conservative partisan cycles in the macroeconomy. Conservative presidencies, for example, tend to emphasize minimal government involvement in the economy and macroeconomic policies that emphasize low, stable inflation. Liberal presidencies tend to adopt more activist government macroeconomic policies that emphasize low unemployment as the primary objective.

Table 1.2 summarizes the connections among the macroeconomic perspectives, political ideologies, political party preferences, and the roles of government versus market forces.

Table 1.2 Classical view versus Keynesian view

Macroeconomic perspective	Political ideology	Political party affiliation	Impact of market forces	Government economic activism	Partisan macroeconomic priority
Classical view	American political conservatism (also libertarianism)	Republican party	Market forces generally efficient, if unimpeded by government	Government failure that worsens the economy	Low inflation emphasis
Keynesian view	American political liberalism	Democratic party	Periodic market failures, such as recessions	Government activism can remedy market failures	Low unemployment emphasis

Median Voter Model and Political Business Cycle Effects

Chapter 5 looks at the theory of rational voter behavior and the median voter model. This framework addresses the interaction among voters and policymakers. The model asserts that government actions (including macroeconomic policy) tend to align with the median voter's most preferred political outcome. This occurs through vote-maximizing economic policies adopted by politicians and political parties. We discuss the assumptions and realism of the median voter model.

Chapters 6 and 7 examine political influence on macroeconomic policy and the business cycle. The two main political business cycle (PBC) effects are the electoral cycle and the partisan cycle. The electoral cycle effect occurs from presidential manipulation of macroeconomic policy to create an economic boom in an election year as an attempt to increase reelection votes. The partisan cycle refers to the effects of the differing macroeconomic preferences of the left and right political parties on the business cycle.

Chapter 8 examines inflation and unemployment in the U.S. economy for evidence of the two PBC effects during the period from 1961 to 2016. The results suggest that the partisan cycle tended to occur during Democratic presidencies. Macroeconomic outcomes during most Republican administrations, on the other hand, were more compatible with the electoral cycle.

Chapter 9 considers some additional issues on the American political macroeconomy. For example, one key assumption of the partisan and electoral cycle theories is that the president can manipulate the macroeconomic policy. We consider the realism of this assumption. We likewise discuss the predictability of macroeconomic performance in response to stabilization policy. We also discuss the issue of independence of the Fed.

Chapter 10 surveys the subject of economic influence on voter behavior and some measures of citizen sentiment. We consider macroeconomic influence on the presidential vote, the congressional vote, and presidential approval. We also discuss economic influence on measures of public opinion and behavior such as macropartisanship, the voter participation rate, the social happiness index, and consumer sentiment.

Chapter 11 then examines some international aspects of the political macroeconomy. We consider the political economy of free trade versus protectionism. We also discuss the three international ideological perspectives of economic liberalism, neomercantilism, and structuralism. Finally, Chapter 12 summarizes the main ideas of this book and provides concluding remarks on the American political macroeconomy.

CHAPTER 2

Refresher on Macroeconomic Measurements and the Business Cycle

Introduction

This chapter reviews the importance of some of the main macroeconomic indicators. Some of the main macroeconomic measurements include inflation, unemployment, interest rates, and gross domestic product (GDP) along with the GDP components. The business cycle is also a key characteristic of macroeconomic performance. Additionally, this chapter discusses Okun's law, which expresses the inverse correlation between unemployment and GDP.

Inflation

The inflation rate is the average percentage rate of change in prices during a time period, such as one year. The Bureau of Labor Statistics (BLS) estimates various types of inflation. Three common measures of inflation relate to the average price of consumer products, the average price of producer goods, and the average price of all products in the economy. The inflation rate equals the percentage rate of change in the corresponding price index. The price index is an estimate of the average price level of goods. The Consumer Price Index (CPI) is a measure of the average price of consumer products. The Producer Price Index (PPI) is a measure of the average price of goods that producers purchase. The GDP deflator is a measure of the average price of all products in the economy. For example, the CPI was 244.028 in Jan 2017 and 249.245 in Jan 2018. Over that one-year time frame, the inflation rate for consumer products was 2.14 percent $= 100 \times (249.245 - 244.028)/244.028$

Consumer product inflation has been mild in the U.S. economy since the early 1980s, typically at a rate of less than 5 percent. Low inflation is called creeping inflation, walking inflation, or mild inflation. In contrast, hyperinflation is extreme inflation of 1,000 percent or more in a one-year period. Hyperinflation occurs from massive printing of money by the central bank. Hyperinflation arises from monetization (printing money) to pay off high government debt.

Generally, inflation occurs when the central bank expands money supply at a rate that is substantially greater than real economic growth. With hyperinflation, money supply growth occurs at a percentage rate of many hundreds or even thousands of times greater than real economic growth. Hyperinflation causes economic breakdown, often leading to recession or even a depression. Business production declines because of extremely high and unstable inflation. Business calculations become difficult and risky under conditions of hyperinflation. This leads to inefficiency and reduced economic activity.

Another category of high inflation that is not as severe as hyperinflation is called galloping inflation. An inflation rate of 100 percent per year is an example of galloping inflation. Both galloping inflation and hyperinflation occur from excessive printing of money by the central bank.

Disinflation is another type of inflationary effect. This refers to a declining inflation rate. Disinflation, for example, occurs if inflation falls from 5 percent to 3 percent. Deflation is an alternative term that is sometimes used to mean the same thing as disinflation. However, a more correct usage of the term "deflation" refers to an overall decline in the average price level or in other words negative inflation. For example, deflation takes place if inflation falls from 3 percent to -1 percent. Average prices become cheaper if deflation arises. Deflation does not normally occur in a growing economy with increasing demand for goods. Expanding demand for products pulls prices upward.

Nominal GDP versus Real GDP

A widely used indicator of overall national economic performance is GDP. This is the total production of new goods and services in the economy.

GDP equals the sum of economic expenditures on new final goods and services across all industries and throughout all geographic regions in a country. GDP in the United States is estimated quarterly and annually by the Bureau of Economic Analysis (BEA).

GDP is estimated nominally and in real terms. Nominal GDP (NGDP) is the dollar value of all new production based on the prices of the new products that are bought and sold. NGDP equals the quantity of all new final products multiplied by the prices of the products.

Real GDP (RGDP), on the other hand, corrects for the distorting effect of changes in product prices. NGDP tends to rise over time. This occurs based on two factors. NGDP rises partly because of more production of goods and services, and partly because of increasing product prices, which is inflation.

RGDP adjusts for the distorting effect of inflation on the measurement for total production in the economy. RGDP is basically a quantity measure for the total amount of new final goods and services. Mathematically, RGDP equals NGDP divided by the average price level (price index) of new goods and services. The price index for the whole economy is called the GDP deflator. Expressed alternatively, NGDP equals the average price of new products (GDP deflator) multiplied by the quantity of new products (RGDP).

$$RGDP = NGDP \div GDP \text{ deflator}$$

or

$$NGDP = GDP \text{ deflator} \times RGDP$$

If NGDP is $20 trillion and the price index is 150, then RGDP is $13.33 trillion (=$20/1.5). To calculate RGDP, the price index is converted into decimal format so that 150 becomes 1.5.

GDP growth is the percentage rate of change in the GDP level over time. Just as the GDP level is measured in nominal terms and real terms, GDP growth is also measured nominally and in real terms. RGDP growth provides a better measure of economic strength than NGDP growth. Analogous to the RGDP level, RGDP growth discounts for the distorting effect of inflation. RGDP growth equals NGDP growth minus inflation:

$$RGDP \text{ growth} = NGDP \text{ growth} - \text{inflation}$$

or

$$NGDP \text{ growth} = RGDP \text{ growth} + \text{inflation}$$

Suppose NGDP growth is 6 percent. This is the percentage growth in new expenditures as measured by the prices of products. Now assume product prices rise by 6 percent. RGDP growth is zero. The 6 percent increase in NGDP is fully attributable to the 6 percent rise in prices. In this case, the amount of new goods and services produced in the economy is unchanged. As a further example, suppose inflation is 2 percent and NGDP growth is 6 percent. RGDP growth is consequently equal to 4 percent. Production of new goods rises by 4 percent, while prices increase by 2 percent.

RGDP growth is the percentage change in the quantity of new goods and services in the economy. Positive RGDP growth indicates an expanding or growing economy. Negative RGDP growth indicates a contracting economy, usually associated with an economic recession.

Potential RGDP and the RGDP gap are two more indicators of economic performance. Potential RGDP is the level of output that occurs if the macroeconomy is operating at potential capacity and efficiency corresponding to full usage of all economic resources, including full employment of labor and capital. The RGDP gap, on the other hand, is the percentage difference between potential RGDP and the actual RGDP.

$$RGDP \text{ Gap} = 100 \times (Potential \text{ } RGDP - Actual \text{ } RGDP) \div Potential \text{ } RGDP$$

If potential RGDP is $20 trillion and actual RGDP is $19 trillion, then the RGDP gap is 5 percent ($= 100 \times (20 - 19)/20$). This signifies 5 percent inefficiency. Alternatively, suppose the economy is operating at potential RGDP so that labor utilization is at full employment. Actual RGDP is equal to potential RGDP in this case, and the RGDP gap is zero. The economy is efficient.

In a sluggish economy, the RGDP gap is a positive value. This occurs because actual RGDP is less than potential RGDP. If actual RGDP is temporarily greater than potential RGDP, then an overheated economy occurs. The RGDP gap is negative in this instance. An overheated economy tends to cause higher inflation because a strong macroeconomic demand drives up prices. A negative RGDP gap, however, is a temporary phenomenon and cannot be sustained. Potential RGDP is the maximum level of RGDP than can be maintained over an extended period of time. Actual RGDP can only occur above potential RGDP for a relatively short time span, perhaps one year or so, until market forces cause actual RGDP to adjust downward to the potential level.

Components of GDP

GDP equals the sum of four main components of macroeconomic activity. The four sectors are consumption expenditure (C), gross domestic private investment (I), government spending (G), and net exports (NX).

$$GDP = C + I + G + NX$$

Table 2.1 NGDP and its four components.

This table shows NGDP in billions of dollars. Each of the components and subcomponents of NGDP is shown in the table. For example, during the third quarter of 2014, NGDP was about $17.6 trillion ($17,599.8 billion). Of this total amount, consumer spending was about $12 trillion, investment was about $2.9 trillion, the level of net exports was about −$0.517 trillion, and government expenditure was about $3.21 trillion.

Consumer Spending and the Consumption Function

The largest component of NGDP is personal consumption expenditures. This is also referred to as consumption or consumer spending. This sector makes up nearly 70 percent of GDP in the U.S. economy (0.68 = $12 trillion/$17.6 trillion). Consumption is made up of three subsectors: durable goods, nondurable goods, and services. Durable goods are products that tend to last for a relatively long period of time. Some examples

Table 2.1 Components of nominal GDP

	2012	2013	III 2013	IV 2013	I 2014	II 2014	III 2014
GDP (measured in billions of dollars)							
Gross domestic product	16,163.2	16,768.1	16,872.3	17,078.3	17,044	17,328.2	17,599.8
Personal consumption expenditures	11,083.1	11,484.3	11,518.7	11,653.3	11,728.5	11,870.7	12,002
Goods	3,741.9	3,851.2	3,865.3	3,886.1	3,890.6	3,964.5	4,011.5
Durable goods	1,192.1	1,249.3	1,252.4	1,261.5	1,262.3	1,298.4	1,320.2
Nondurable goods	2,549.8	2,601.9	2,612.9	2,624.6	2,628.4	2,666.1	2,691.3
Services	7,341.3	7,633.2	7,653.4	7,767.2	7,837.8	7,906.2	7,990.4
Gross private domestic investment	2,479.2	2,648	2,708.9	2,745.2	2,714.4	2,843.6	2,905.1
Fixed investment	2,414.3	2,573.9	2,598.1	2,654.6	2,674.3	2,743.4	2,810.6
Nonresidential	1,972	2,054	2,060.2	2,118.7	2,134.6	2,191.2	2,244.3
Structures	446.9	457.2	463	481.7	487.9	504.4	513.3
Equipment	904.1	949.7	948.8	980	979.5	1,008.6	1,038.2
Intellectual property products	621	647.1	648.4	657	667.2	678.2	692.7
Residential	442.3	519.9	538	535.9	539.7	552.2	566.4
Change in private inventories	64.9	74.1	110.7	90.5	40.1	100.3	94.5
Net exports of goods and services	−568.3	−508.2	−509.9	−462.9	−538	−549.2	−516.5
Exports	2,194.2	2,262.2	2,268.4	2,324.6	2,284.7	2,344.3	2,366.5
Goods	1,527.2	1,562.8	1,565.7	1,614	1,575.3	1,623.3	1,645
Services	667	699.4	702.7	710.7	709.5	721.1	721.4
Imports	2,762.5	2,770.4	2,778.3	2,787.5	2,822.7	2,893.5	2,883
Goods	2,306	2,302.3	2,308.6	2,309.7	2,341.5	2,405.6	2,393.7
Services	456.4	468.1	469.7	477.8	481.2	487.9	489.3
Government consumption expenditures	3,169.2	3,143.9	3,154.7	3,142.7	3,139.1	3,163.1	3,209.3
Federal	1,291.4	1,231.5	1,233.9	1,216.2	1,208.1	1,210.5	1,241.3
National defense	818	769.9	774.9	757.5	749.9	754.6	784
Nondefense	473.4	461.6	459	458.7	458.2	455.9	457.3
State and local	1,877.8	1,912.4	1,920.7	1,926.5	1,931	1,952.6	1,968

Source: BEA

include automobiles, household appliances, furniture, and computers. Nondurable goods are perishable products. Examples of nondurable goods include food, clothing, and gasoline.

Services consist of consumer spending on activities or assistance received rather than spending on material products. Examples of consumer services include watching a movie in a theater, education in schools, and getting a haircut. Services are the largest subsector of consumer expenditures. The U.S. economy is sometimes referred to as a service economy.

The most important determinant of consumption spending is disposable income. Disposable income is the level of household income available for spending and saving after all taxes are subtracted and all government transfers (such as social security and unemployment benefits) are added. The part of disposable income that is not spent goes to saving. The greater the level of income, the higher the amount of consumer spending. The lower the level of income, the smaller the amount of consumer expenditures.

The relation between consumption and disposable income exhibits a stable linear pattern and is called the consumption function. This is illustrated in Figure 2.1.

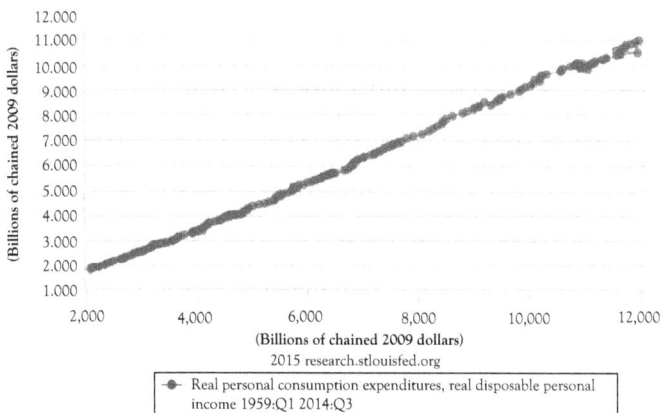

Figure 2.1 Consumption function

Source: Federal Reserve Economic Data (FRED)

Consumer spending is depicted along the vertical axis, and disposable income is displayed along the horizontal axis. The chart shows an upward-sloping effect for consumer spending relative to income. Higher disposable income leads to more consumer spending. In addition to income, some other determinants that affect consumer spending are wealth, household debt, and consumer confidence.

Economic Investment versus Financial Investment

Economic investment versus financial investment are two distinct ways of thinking about investment. These two classifications of investment are sometimes confused with each other. The two categories of investment are distinct but indirectly related. Economic investment is directly included in the GDP calculation and is referred to as gross private domestic investment. Financial investment, on the other hand, is not a part of GDP. However, financial investment functions as a major source of funds used by firms to purchase economic investment in tools, capital equipment, factories, etc.

Financial investment consists of financial assets that serve as a store of wealth from a saving perspective. Some examples of financial investment include stocks, bonds, government securities, and bank account deposits. The main purpose of financial investment from a saving point of view is to increase income and wealth through interest earnings, dividends, and capital gains.

From a business perspective, economic investment or real investment is the use of funds associated with financial investment for the purpose of buying new plant, equipment, and tools to increase production capacity. Businesses, for example, sell stocks and bonds to the public as a source of funds to buy plant and equipment. Economic investment is an economic resource, along with labor and natural resources. Financial investment is not a resource but a source of funding that is used to purchase the resource of economic investment.

Gross Private Domestic Investment and Investment Demand

Gross private domestic investment is an important component of GDP that affects future economic growth. Investment, however, is a smaller component of GDP than the larger sector of consumption expenditures. Additionally, economic investment fluctuates up and down to a greater degree than consumer spending. Economic investment is often considered the engine for economic growth. Investment directly affects production capacity. If economic investment is strong, the total amount of capital stock resource in the economy rises. This adds to the production potential of the economy. If economic investment is high, the capital stock increases substantially, and the economy grows rapidly. If investment is low, the capital stock rises slowly. The economy consequently grows slowly or may contract. The total capital stock equals the accumulation of economic investment over time, excluding the effects of depreciation (the wearing out) of capital. Similarly, economic investment equals the change in the total capital stock, excluding the effects of depreciation.

Figure 2.2 shows the up-and-down pattern of real economic investment in relation to RGDP in the U.S. economy.

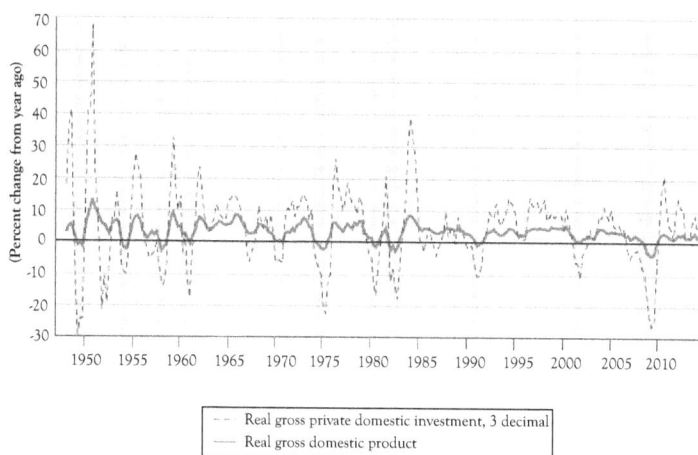

Figure 2.2 Relation between gross private domestic investment and GDP

Source: FRED

The dashed line is the economic investment growth rate, while the solid line is RGDP growth. The graph shows that a strong level of investment tends to pull economic growth upward. A low level of investment drags RGDP growth downward, sometimes into the recession range of negative RGDP growth. The vertical shaded regions in the graph are periods of economic recession.

Total private domestic investment consists of three main types of expenditures, as expressed in Table 2.1. They are nonresidential investment (or business investment), residential investment, and the change in business inventories. Business investment refers to new plant, equipment, factories, other construction, and tools that are used by firms in the production of goods and services. Residential investment is construction of housing, apartments, and other residential structures. The change in business inventories is also included in investment. Inventories refer to unsold goods that firms intend to sell. The change in inventories often rises if businesses sell less than expected. This is frequently a signal that the economy is growing less than anticipated. The change in inventories often decreases if sales are greater than predicted. This often suggests the economy is growing faster than anticipated.

A major determinant of economic investment is interest rates. Interest rates adversely affect business and residential investment. Higher interest rates mean higher borrowing costs. Economic investment consequently declines. Firms borrow less funds for purchases of new plant and equipment as borrowing costs rise. Lower interest rates mean lower borrowing costs. Economic investment and economic growth consequently tend to rise. Firms borrow more funds at lower borrowing costs to purchase more plant and equipment. The relation between economic investment and the interest rate is sometimes called the investment demand relation.

Figure 2.3 shows the inverse correlation between the AAA corporate bond interest rate and economic investment.

The AAA corporate bond rate is measured along the vertical axis, and the real gross domestic investment is indicated along the horizontal axis. The downward pattern of the data, although not perfectly correlated, shows a general inverse correlation between the interest rate and investment. The downward-sloping line is a rough approximation of the investment demand curve. The reason that all the data points do not perfectly occur on the investment demand line is because other factors also affect investment. Some of the other factors are profitability, business expectations, technology, taxes, and government regulation of business.

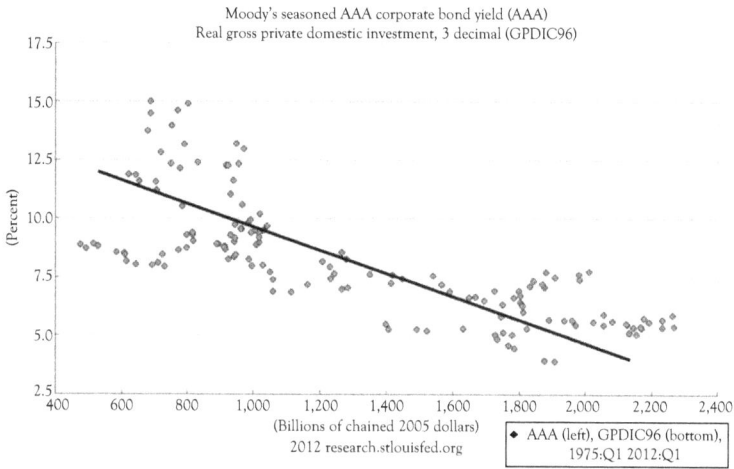

Figure 2.3 *Relation between investment and the interest rate*

Source: FRED

Government Expenditures

Government expenditures make up almost one-fifth of GDP ($0.18 = 3.21/17.6$ from Table 2.1). The largest category of government spending at the federal level is military purchases. Some examples of government spending at the state and local levels are public education, law enforcement, and social welfare. Government spending also includes health care expenditures, including the Medicaid and Medicare programs.

One category of government activity that is not directly included in GDP is government transfer programs. This is because no direct government purchases are involved. Transfer payments consist of the flow or redistribution of funds from taxpayers to transfer recipients. Transfers do not appear in GDP until the transfer income is spent on consumer goods and services by the recipients.

Social security is an example of a transfer program because the activity involves a transfer of income from wage earners in the form of a tax. The funds are redistributed to retirees in the form of retirement income. If social security recipients spend their social security income on new goods, such as food and clothing, then this economic activity is included in GDP as consumption expenditure.

For many nations, government spending makes up a larger share of GDP than the United States. This occurs because many countries such as Canada and the countries of Western Europe have a more expansive system of government-provided health care than the United States. The issue of government spending and the corresponding issue of taxation and their impact on the economy is called fiscal policy, which will be discussed in Chapter 4.

Net Exports or the Trade Balance

Net exports is also referred to as the trade balance. Net exports are the fourth category of GDP. Net exports (NX) equal total exports (X) minus total imports (M). Since the mid-1970s, the level of net exports in the United States has been negative. This indicates a trade deficit. Table 2.1 shows that the trade deficit was −516.5 billion dollars in the third quarter of 2014. Of this amount, total exports of goods and services were 2.3665 trillion dollars, while total imports were 2.883 trillion dollars ($NX = X − M = −0.5165$ trillion dollars = 2.3665 trillion dollars minus 2.883 trillion dollars).

Some other indicators of international economic activity besides the trade balance include exchange rates, international investments, and the balance of payments. These international economic considerations are not directly included in GDP.

Unemployment

The unemployment rate is an estimate for the percentage of the labor force who are jobless. Unemployed persons do not currently have jobs, but are actively seeking work through job applications, resumes, interviews, and so forth. The total labor force equals the sum of all persons who are working either full time or part-time plus the number of individuals who are unemployed.

The unemployment rate excludes people who are outside of the labor force. The out-of-the-labor-force category consists of individuals who are unable to work for various reasons plus people who are capable of work but who decide not to seek employment. Some examples of persons who are out-of-the labor force are retired individuals, stay-at-home parents, children, institutionalized or disabled persons who are unable to work, and individuals in prisons.

Approximately half of the population in the United States is in the labor force, while about half of the population is out of the labor force. The unemployment rate, as estimated by the BLS, probably underestimates the full extent of the unemployment problem. The BLS unemployment calculation, for example, does not consider the effects of underemployment and discouraged workers.

Underemployment refers to people who are working part time but who prefer to work full time if the opportunity occurs. Additionally, the unemployment rate does not consider whether employees are working in their preferred occupations or not. Discouraged workers, on the other hand, consist of people who are jobless but who gave up actively searching for work because of low prospects. Discouraged workers are excluded from the unemployment statistic until they begin actively searching for jobs.

Natural Unemployment Rate: Structural Unemployment plus Frictional Unemployment

The economy is at full efficiency and peak capacity at potential GDP if all economic resources including labor are employed and effectively utilized. Full employment of labor does not mean the unemployment rate is zero. Even in a best-case scenario, some unemployment is inevitable because of job firings and job quits. These are people who are temporarily out of work and between jobs.

Full employment of labor corresponds to what is called the natural unemployment rate. This is equal to approximately 5 percent in the United States. The natural unemployment rate is the efficient level of unemployment. The natural rate of unemployment is often referred to as NAIRU. This stands for the nonaccelerating inflation rate of unemployment.

The natural unemployment rate equals the sum of two subcategories of unemployment. They are structural unemployment plus frictional unemployment. Structural unemployment equals about 2½ percent.

Frictional unemployment also equals about 2½ percent. This yields a natural unemployment rate of about 5 percent.

$$\text{Natural Unemployment} = \text{Structural Unemployment} \\ + \text{Frictional Unemployment}$$

Structural unemployment is the percentage of the labor force who are jobless because of insufficient job skills relative to the employment opportunities available. Lack of proficiency in reading, writing, math, and computer skills, and insufficient education or training are among the main causes of structural unemployment.

Because of intense competition in the global economy, many semiskilled workers in manufacturing industries have lost jobs as domestic factories have closed and relocated to developing countries with cheaper wages. Some laid-off factory workers fall under the category of structural unemployment if they lack work skills to be reemployed in other jobs. Structurally unemployed individuals sometimes experience long-term joblessness. Some structurally unemployed persons may face long periods of time without work, until they attain the necessary occupation skills to regain employment.

Besides structural unemployment, the other category of unemployment is frictional. This type of unemployment corresponds to people who are temporarily out of work because of firings or job quits. However, structurally unemployed persons possess sufficient job skills to be rehired in a relatively short period of time, usually within a few weeks or a few months. Frictional unemployment has one beneficial effect. Frictional unemployment can contribute to labor productivity. Frictional unemployment signifies flexibility in the labor market. Frictional unemployment helps facilitate a better match between employers and employees. This promotes greater labor productivity and more efficiency.

Frictional unemployment refers to individuals who either quit or are fired, but subsequently are rehired within a short time. Consequently, frictionally unemployed persons may obtain a better fit with the next employer in terms of job requirements and career interests. The greater the compatibility between the employee and the employer, the higher the labor productivity and economic efficiency in the workplace.

Cyclical Unemployment or the Unemployment Gap

If the actual unemployment rate ends up being higher than the natural unemployment rate, then the labor market and the economy are in a state of inefficiency. The gap between actual unemployment and natural unemployment is called cyclical unemployment or the unemployment gap.

Cyclical unemployment is a measure of the amount of slack or inefficiency in the labor market. Suppose the actual unemployment rate is 7 percent while the natural unemployment rate is 5 percent. In this case, cyclical unemployment is 2 percent. Alternatively, suppose the economy is operating efficiently at the natural unemployment rate of 5 percent. In this instance, the unemployment gap and cyclical unemployment are zero.

The actual unemployment rate equals the sum of structural unemployment, frictional unemployment, and cyclical unemployment.

$$\text{Actual Unemployment} = \text{Natural Unemployment} + \text{Cyclical Unemployment}$$
$$= \text{Structural Unemployment} + \text{Frictional Unemployment} + \text{Cyclical Unemployment}$$

or

$$\text{Cyclical Unemployment} = \text{Actual Unemployment} - \text{Natural Unemployment} = \text{Unemployment Gap}$$

Business Cycle

The business cycle is the up-and-down pattern of macroeconomic performance over time. Business cycle fluctuations may be expressed in terms of various indicators, such as the level of RGDP, the RGDP growth rate, unemployment, or even inflation and interest rates.

Figure 2.4 shows the general business cycle pattern in terms of the RGDP level over time.

The wavelike pattern, as shown by the curved line, depicts business cycle fluctuations. The up-and-down movement of economic performance consists of three main parts. They are economic expansions, economic recessions, and the economic growth trend or the secular growth

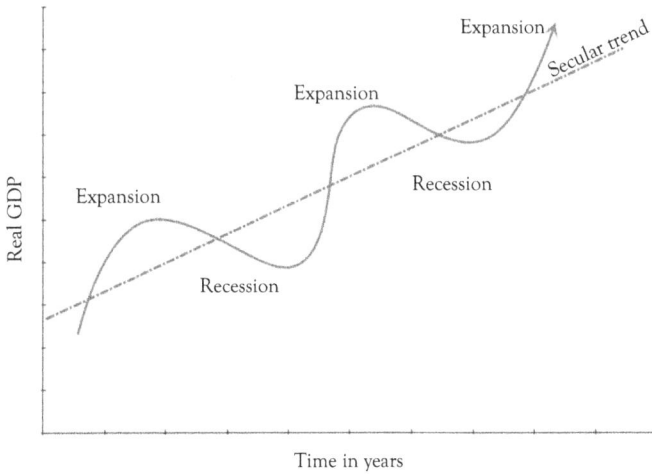

Figure 2.4 Business cycle pattern

trend. Periods of upward movement in RGDP indicate economic expansions. Episodes of declining RGDP signify economic contractions or recessions. An economic expansion occurs if RGDP is rising. An economic recession occurs if RGDP is declining. In the U.S. economy, expansions often last for 5 to 6 years or sometimes longer. Economic recessions occur for shorter durations of time, frequently between 1 and 2 years.

The secular trend is the upward-sloping straight line. This indicates the average growth rate for the economy. In the U.S. economy, the average RGDP growth rate is about 2½ percent per year. This upward trend of economic growth occurs because of advancements in commercial technology as well as from increasing economic resources such as labor and capital. In subsequent chapters, we consider the issue of political influences on the business cycle.

Figure 2.5 shows the actual business cycle pattern for the United States in terms of RGDP growth and the unemployment rate. These two macroeconomic variables are measured along the vertical axis in the chart. The unemployment rate is shown as the dashed line, while RGDP growth is shown as the solid line. Time in years from 1965 to 2014 is measured along the horizontal axis. The shaded regions are periods of economic recession, while the other time periods are associated with economic expansion.

The chart shows up-and-down variations in RGDP growth and unemployment. Periods of high RGDP growth are often associated with

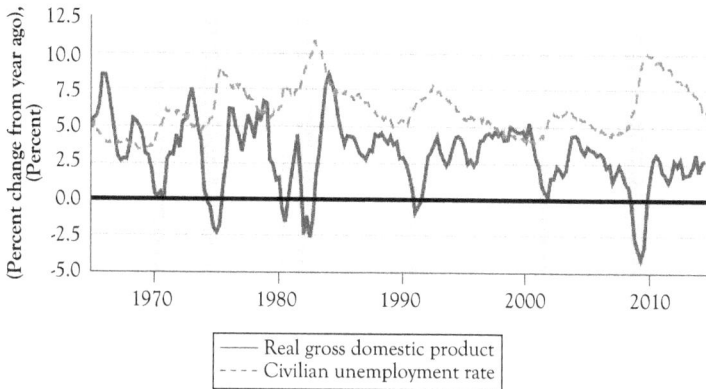

Figure 2.5 *Unemployment and RGDP growth*

Source: FRED

declining unemployment. When economic growth is strong, firms tend to hire more workers to produce more goods. The unemployment rate consequently declines. Periods of low RGDP growth often occur in the gray-shaded regions in the graph. This depicts economic recessions and rising unemployment. When economic growth is weak, firms employ fewer workers because of reduced production of goods and services. Therefore, unemployment tends to worsen.

Okun's Law

A positive unemployment gap (positive cyclical unemployment) occurs if actual unemployment is greater than natural unemployment. Correspondingly, actual GDP is likely to be less than potential GDP. The correlation between unemployment and GDP is called Okun's law. This is named after the late economist Arthur Okun. Okun's law is the inverse correlation between RGDP growth and the change in the unemployment rate. When GDP growth rises, unemployment tends to fall and vice versa.

Figure 2.6 shows Okun's law in terms of RGDP growth and the change in unemployment rate.

RGDP growth is measured along the vertical axis, while the change in the unemployment rate is shown along the horizontal axis. The downward-sloping line depicts the inverse correlation between the change in unemployment and real RGDP growth. Although the empirical

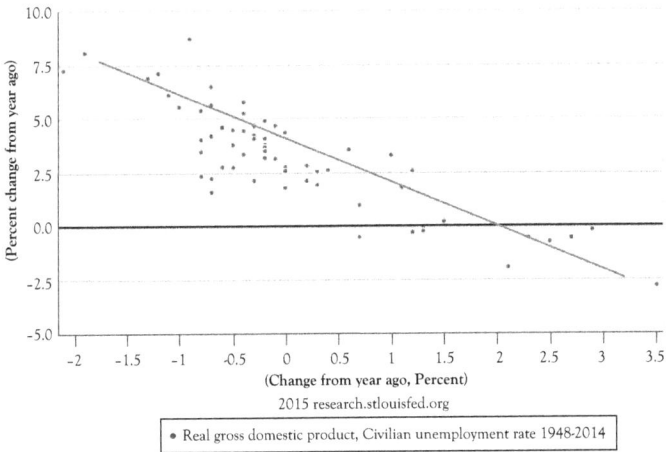

Figure 2.6 Okun's law

Source: FRED

correlation is not exact, the chart shows a general pattern of declining RGDP growth alongside periods of rising unemployment. The unemployment rate and real economic growth tend to move in opposite directions.

Okun's law may also be expressed in terms of the GDP gap and unemployment. The greater the GDP gap (the percentage difference between potential GDP and actual GDP), the higher the unemployment rate. Figure 2.7 illustrates this effect. The figure shows a line chart of potential GDP, actual GDP, and the unemployment rate from 2002 to 2014.

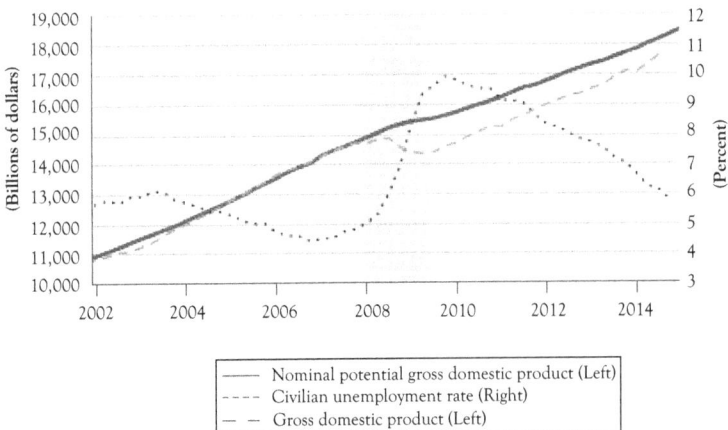

Figure 2.7 GDP gap and unemployment

Source: FRED

The solid line is potential GDP, the dashed line is actual GDP, and the dotted line is unemployment. The gray-shaded region is the Great Recession from December 2007 to June 2009. Prior to the Great Recession, the dashed line was approximately even with the solid line, indicating an efficient economy. The GDP gap was approximately zero. Alongside this GDP effect, unemployment declined as shown by the decreasing dotted line. During this period, business firms hired more workers to produce more goods associated with a strong GDP.

Prior to the Great Recession, actual unemployment fell to about 4½ percent, which is below the natural unemployment rate of around 5 percent. This unemployment outcome indicates macroeconomic overheating. An unemployment rate that falls below the natural unemployment rate because of a strong macroeconomic demand cannot be sustained and will likely lead to rising inflation. Figure 2.8 shows the pattern of inflation in association with actual GDP and potential GDP.

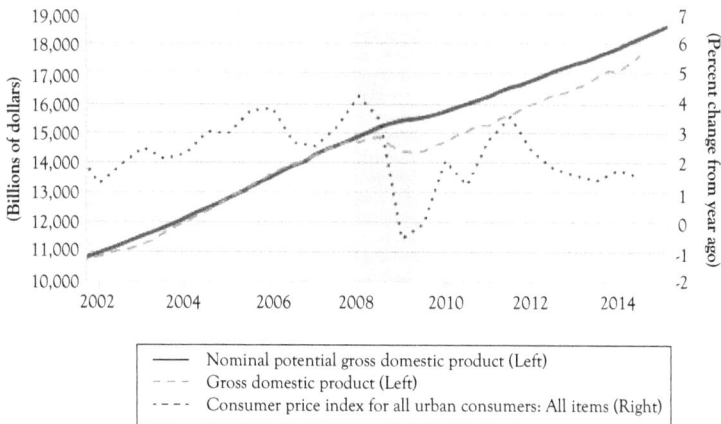

Figure 2.8 GDP gap and inflation

Source: FRED

The dashed and solid lines once again denote actual GDP and potential GDP. Additionally, the dotted line is the CPI inflation rate. Prior to the Great Recession, inflation rose from about 2 percent in 2002 to above 4 percent by 2008. This inflationary outcome occurred because of a strong macroeconomic demand, which drove prices upward.

During the Great Recession, the dashed line fell below the solid line. In other words, actual GDP dropped below potential GDP. This indicates a positive GDP gap or a recessionary gap. The inefficiency of the Great Recession was associated with a weak macroeconomic demand and therefore less production of goods and services.

As predicted by Okun's law, unemployment worsened alongside the widening gap between potential GDP and actual GDP. Unemployment, in this period, rose from around 5 percent to nearly 10 percent, as shown in Figure 2.7. During the Great Recession, fewer workers were employed by firms because of the decline in goods and services produced.

In addition, inflation fell as actual GDP dropped below potential GDP during the Great Recession. This recessionary gap led to declining inflation because of lower macroeconomic demand. During the Great Recession, inflation fell from about 4 to −0.5 percent. In other words, deflation briefly occurred during the Great Recession. In the next chapter, we discuss the theoretical interrelation between inflation, unemployment, and RGDP.

CHAPTER 3

Mainstream Macroeconomic Theory and the Expectational Phillips Curve

Introduction

The last chapter discussed some of the main macroeconomic measurements, such as GDP, economic growth, inflation, unemployment, and the business cycle. This chapter examines the theoretical cause–effect relation among those economic indicators. This chapter considers some of the major factors that affect GDP, economic growth, unemployment, inflation, and the business cycle. Basic macroeconomic theory provides a foundation for an examination of political business cycle effects in later chapters.

A model is a mathematical or graphical representation of a theory. Economic models attempt to explain and predict cause–effect patterns among economic variables. Theories or models are not perfect predictors of economic outcomes. Predicting events with precision is often difficult, especially in soft sciences like economics.

Individual actions, including economic behavior, naturally varies from person to person. Economic analyses usually focus on the law of averages across a large sample or a population rather than predicting the economic actions of individuals. Predicting the economic behavior of individuals is problematic because of the wide range of personal tastes and preferences. Predicting average or total economic behavior across a large group is more accurate. Even when considering average or total economic behavior, some margin of error occurs between economic predictions and economic events. A useful theory explains economic outcomes well.

The more useful the theory, the smaller the gap between economic predictions and economic outcomes.

A useful model from a political macroeconomy vantagepoint is the expectational Phillips curve model. This framework explains the relation between inflation and unemployment. The expectational Phillips curve model is relevant to the study of the political macroeconomy because inflation and unemployment are important issues that impact electoral and partisan politics. In electoral politics, inflation and unemployment affect presidential approval, presidential votes, and congressional votes. In partisan politics, inflation and unemployment are important considerations regarding the partisan macroeconomic agendas of the right and left political parties.

The expectational Phillips curve explains the short-run and long-run connection between inflation and unemployment. In the short run, business productivity and resource costs, including labor expenses, are assumed to be constant. Consequently, a short-run trade-off or inverse relation often occurs between inflation and unemployment. If inflation rises, then unemployment tends to decline in the short term. If inflation decreases, then unemployment rises.

In the long term, the economy adjusts to equilibrium through the process of market forces. Unemployment moves to full-employment through supply and demand. Correspondingly, the wage rate and expected inflation adjust to the actual rate of inflation. This is called the self-correcting mechanism of market forces. Full employment occurs at the natural unemployment rate of about five percent in the United States.

An important issue is the length of time needed for the economy to automatically adjust through market forces from a situation of short-run inefficiency to long-run equilibrium at full employment. If the self-correcting mechanism of market forces is slow in adjusting to full employment, then government policy in the form of fiscal and monetary measures may be called on to remedy macroeconomic weakness. If market forces occur efficiently in a timely manner to remedy unemployment, then macroeconomic policy is unnecessary and could be counterproductive.

The political right sees market forces as generally efficient. The political right normally adheres to the idea that the economy adjusts quickly from inefficiency to full employment through market forces. Macroeconomic policy intervention should therefore be minimal. The political left sees market forces as sometimes inefficient. The political left views the economy as sometimes adjusting slowly from inefficiency to full employment through market forces. The political left tends to support activist macroeconomic policies.

In addition to the expectational Phillips curve, Okun's law is an important macroeconomic relation. Okun's law is the inverse correlation between real economic growth and unemployment. The expectational Phillips curve combined with Okun's law provides a basis for understanding the interconnection between inflation, unemployment, the real GDP level (RGDP), and RGDP growth in the short run and long run.

The economy may be understood as the interaction between two general markets. They are the product market and the resource market. The product market refers to macroeconomic outcomes such as RGDP and product inflation. The product market may be examined using macroeconomic supply and macroeconomic demand. Macroeconomic demand is also called aggregate demand, while macroeconomic supply is also referred to as aggregate supply.

The resource market refers to the three main economic resources or factors of production. They are land or natural resources, labor, and capital. Many macroeconomic theories, including the expectational Phillips curve, emphasize the labor market. The labor market consists of labor supply and labor demand. Labor market outcomes include worker wages and the unemployment rate. Figure 3.1 shows the circular flow of the resource market and the product market in the economy.

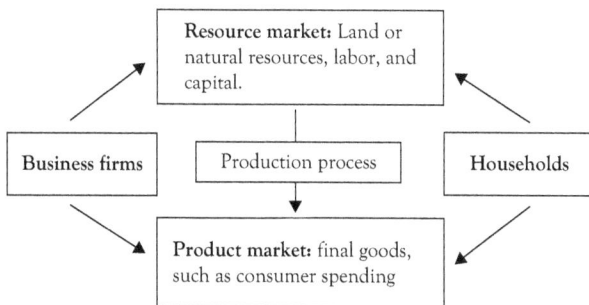

Figure 3.1 Circular flow of the product market and the resource market

In the resource market, business firms employ economic resources, such as labor. Households supply economic resources, such as labor, to business firms in the resource market. Households receive resource payments from business firms, such as wages for work supplied. Business firms produce and supply goods and services to households in the product market. In the product market, households purchase products, such as consumer goods, from business firms. Households buy economic goods and services based on product prices and income.

Firms supply goods in the product market and demand or hire labor in the resource market. Households demand goods in the product market and supply labor in the resource market. In the resource market, money flows from firms to households in the form of worker wages and income. In the product market, money flows from households to firms in the form of product prices and sales revenue.

Macroeconomic Efficiency versus Inefficiency

Market forces are an important consideration in the political macroeconomy. Market forces consist of the summation and synergy of commercial transactions between buyers and sellers in the private sector of the economy. Government economic activity is also an important consideration. This includes government spending, taxes, government rules and regulations, and the monetary policy by the Federal Reserve. Government economic activity is not a direct element of market forces. Government activity, however, impacts the market forces of supply and demand. For example, the government hires employees in the labor market and purchases goods in the product market.

The market mechanism of demand and supply occurs as buyers and sellers interact and exchange money for economic goods and services through the price mechanism. Economic efficiency occurs at equilibrium where supply equals demand. In equilibrium, the amount of a product that buyers want to purchase equals the quantity of economic goods that suppliers wish to sell. For efficiency and equilibrium to come about, the market price for a product must adjust flexibly so that the market clears. If an economic market is efficient, then the price of a good adjusts so that the quantity supplied of the product equals the quantity demanded of the product. Neither shortage nor surplus takes place in an efficient market. For the whole economy, efficiency occurs if economic resources are employed in a least-cost method of production that supplies the best combination of goods and services to meet the economic demands of society. This is called allocative efficiency.

For efficiency and long-run macroeconomic equilibrium to happen, prices in the product market and wages in the labor market must occur at equilibrium where supply equals demand. This takes place if actual GDP equals potential GDP in the product market, while at the same time the actual unemployment rate equals the natural unemployment rate in the labor market. Both the unemployment gap and the GDP gap are equal to zero in an efficient economy. As discussed in Chapter 2, the unemployment gap is the difference between actual unemployment and the natural unemployment rate, while the GDP gap is the difference between actual GDP and potential GDP.

A short-run macroeconomic outcome signifies inefficiency in the labor and product markets. In the short run, the economy is not at natural unemployment and potential GDP. The GDP gap and the unemployment gap are non-zero. Two kinds of macroeconomic inefficiency may occur. They are insufficient macroeconomic demand and excess macroeconomic demand.

A recessionary gap occurs from insufficient macroeconomic demand. A shortage of goods takes place in the product market, while a surplus of labor (high unemployment) arises in the labor market. The economy experiences low growth, perhaps a recession. Actual GDP is less than potential, while unemployment is greater than the natural rate.

The other type of macroeconomic inefficiency is an inflationary gap. An inflationary gap occurs from excess macroeconomic demand. This arises if unemployment is less than the natural rate and GDP is greater than potential. An inflationary gap tends to cause rising inflation. A GDP level that is greater than potential output cannot be sustained and causes macroeconomic overheating. Excessive demand in the macroeconomy pulls product prices upward.

Table 3.1 summarizes the characteristics of long-run macroeconomic efficiency and the two types of short-run inefficiency.

Table 3.1 Long-run and short-run macroeconomic outcomes

Economic markets	Long-run equilibrium: macroeconomic demand equals macroeconomic supply	Short-run disequilibrium: insufficient macroeconomic demand	Short-run disequilibrium: excess macroeconomic demand
Product market	Actual GDP equals potential GDP	Recessionary gap: actual GDP is less than potential GDP	Inflationary gap: actual GDP is greater than potential GDP
Labor market	Unemployment rate equals the natural unemployment rate	Unemployment is greater than the natural rate	Unemployment is less than the natural rate

Macroeconomic Supply and Demand

The theory of aggregate supply and demand is a useful way to understand macroeconomic outcomes in the product market such as GDP and product price inflation. Aggregate demand relates to expenditure patterns among the four main components of GDP. The four components of GDP are consumption, investment, net exports, and government purchases. The determinants that affect demand for any of the four GDP components also impact overall macroeconomic demand. For example, suppose consumption increases because of the determinant of optimistic consumer sentiment. Macroeconomic demand also expands because consumer spending is a component of GDP.

Macroeconomic supply involves factors that impact production and pricing from a business firm perspective. Some examples of macroeconomic supply determinants are resource availability, production costs, resource productivity, and government intervention in the business sector. Some types of government intervention are business taxes, business subsidies, and government regulations on business. As an example of a supply-side effect, suppose production costs go up, such as higher energy prices. Macroeconomic supply consequently declines. Business firms reduce employment and production. This occurs as a cost-cutting device to partially offset the higher production expenses.

Short-run macroeconomic inefficiency may occur from shocks to either macroeconomic demand or macroeconomic supply. Some examples of macroeconomic shocks are major changes in energy prices, bursting of financial bubbles, major natural disasters, inefficient government economic policies, and war. A macroeconomic shock causes unemployment to diverge from the natural rate and actual GDP to deviate from potential. If a macroeconomic shock occurs, worker wages in the labor market become out of sync with changes in product prices in the product market. The labor market is in disequilibrium. However, if wages and prices adjust rapidly and flexibly in the product and labor markets through supply and demand forces, then the economy returns to long-run equilibrium at potential GDP and natural unemployment. If wages and prices do not adjust or respond quickly, then macroeconomic policy may be needed to remedy the inefficiency.

Expected Inflation, Wage Inflation, and Long-Run Equilibrium

Expected inflation is an important concept in modern macroeconomic theory. Expected inflation is the level of inflation that businesses and labor anticipate will occur over the next year or so, based on their best calculations and estimates. Management and labor negotiate with each other to determine worker wages and salaries based on expected inflation. Workers and employers consider expected inflation when forming wage contracts and other labor agreements. For instance, if product prices are expected to rise, then wages would likely rise by a similar amount to compensate. Expected inflation affects what households think they will be able to afford over the next year or so. If workers anticipate high inflation, they will demand higher wages from employers to have enough income to pay for more expensive products. If inflation is expected to be low, workers will be less demanding of higher wages from employers.

Let us assume product inflation is expected to be 3 percent over the next year. Through labor market negotiations and market forces among employers and employees, worker wages also rise by 3 percent (assuming worker productivity is constant). If workers anticipate product inflation will be 3 percent, then they will seek a wage increase of 3 percent to maintain their standard of living. Employers, likewise, are willing to pay the higher wage rate because firms anticipate being able to sell products at higher prices, which yields greater sales revenues. Expected inflation affects business sales forecasts. Based on expected inflation, firms anticipate the level of revenues they will earn. Based on inflationary expectations, firms determine the level of wage they can afford to pay employees.

If expected inflation held by workers and firms is accurate, then expected inflation equals actual inflation. Consequently, the labor and product markets occur in long-run equilibrium. For example, let us once again assume expected inflation and wage inflation are 3 percent. If actual inflation is also 3 percent, then the economy is in long-run equilibrium and efficient. The wage rate occurs at equilibrium, and the labor market clears at natural unemployment. Wage inflation is aligned with product inflation because inflationary expectations are realized. Correspondingly, actual GDP equals potential GDP in the product market.

Unexpected Inflation and Short-Run Outcomes

Inefficiency occurs if inflationary expectations are mistaken or inaccurate. This happens if expected inflation differs from actual inflation. The economy is consequently in a short-run position of inefficiency, such as a recession. Unexpected inflation is the gap between actual inflation and expected inflation. If unexpected inflation is zero, then expected inflation equals actual inflation. The labor and product markets are in long-run equilibrium.

If expected inflation differs from actual inflation, then the labor market and product market are in disequilibrium. Suppose the economy is in short-run disequilibrium. Business and worker expectations about inflation are either higher or lower than actual inflation. Unexpected inflation occurs, and an unemployment gap and a GDP gap take place. The greater the amount of unexpected inflation, the larger the unemployment gap and the GDP gap.

Let us assume actual inflation is less than expected. Negative unexpected inflation occurs. Firms are forced to sell products at a lower price than originally expected. Businesses respond by reducing employment and selling a lesser amount than initially planned. This cost-cutting strategy partially offsets the reduced revenues from lower prices than anticipated. A recessionary gap occurs. Actual unemployment rises above the natural rate and actual GDP falls below potential.

Suppose actual inflation is greater than expected. Positive unexpected inflation develops, and an inflationary gap arises. Higher inflation than expected means firms can sell products at a higher price than originally envisioned. Firms sell more goods at the higher price to earn greater revenues and profits. Businesses expand employment and produce more products than initially planned. This revenue-enhancing strategy of supplying more goods at a higher price generates greater profitability, assuming average production costs are unchanged. Consequently, unemployment falls below the natural rate, and actual GDP rises above potential GDP.

Table 3.2 summarizes the short-run and long-run effects of unexpected inflation.

Table 3.2 Characteristics of long-run and short-run macroeconomic performance

Long-run equilibrium	Short-run inflationary gap	Short-run recessionary gap
Actual inflation equals expected inflation	Actual inflation is greater-than-expected inflation	Actual inflation is less than expected inflation
Zero unexpected inflation	Positive unexpected inflation	Negative unexpected inflation
Worker wages are fully adjusted to product prices	Worker wages are not fully adjusted to product prices; wages must increase to compensate for higher-than-expected prices	Worker wages are not fully adjusted to product prices; firms will reduce real wages to compensate for lower-than-expected prices
Zero unemployment gap	Negative unemployment gap	Positive unemployment gap
Unemployment equals the natural rate	Unemployment less than the natural rate	Unemployment is greater than the natural rate
Labor market in equilibrium	Labor market in disequilibrium	Labor market in disequilibrium
Actual GDP equals potential GDP	Actual GDP is greater than potential GDP.	Actual GDP is less than potential GDP.
Zero GDP gap—product market is in equilibrium	Negative GDP gap— product market is in disequilibrium	Positive GDP gap—product market is in disequilibrium

Self-Correcting Mechanism: Rational Expectations versus Adaptive Expectations

In the long run, the economy experiences full utilization of resources, including full employment in the labor market. If efficient, the economy adjusts from short-run disequilibrium to long-run equilibrium through market forces. This market process is called the self-correcting mechanism. Through market forces, expected inflation adjusts to actual inflation. The wage rate, which is based on expected inflation, adjusts to equilibrium in the labor market. Unemployment moves to the natural unemployment rate as worker wages efficiently adjust to expected inflation and actual inflation. Worker wages, in the long run, adjust to product prices and the labor market moves to equilibrium. Expected inflation and wage inflation, in the long run, align with actual inflation through the self-correcting mechanism.

The speed of adjustment of expected inflation to actual inflation is an important issue. This issue concerns the amount of time required for expected inflation and wages to fully adjust to actual inflation. Two main viewpoints occur on this issue. The first perspective is the classical macroeconomic view and the theoretical construct of rational inflationary expectations. The political right tends to embrace the rational expectations perspective. The other perspective is Keynesianism and the theoretical construct of adaptive expectations. The political left tends to embrace adaptive expectations.

The classical view maintains that the adjustment of expected inflation and wages to actual product inflation to reach long-run equilibrium occurs relatively fast and efficiently through a rational-expectations mechanism. Inflationary expectations held by labor and management are rational and well informed. Expected inflation, on average, equals actual inflation, with only small random differences. Excluding surprise economic shocks, inflationary expectations closely reflect actual inflation.

According to rational expectations, the economy generally occurs in long-run equilibrium or close to it, in the absence of inefficient government policies that create shocks that disrupt economic expectations and economic markets. The classical view maintains that government intervention in the product and labor markets frequently causes inefficiencies and unintended economic consequences. Government economic activism should be minimal. The classical perspective and rational expectations align with the conservative political ideology that argues for a small role of government in the economy.

Besides rational expectations, the other main view on the self-correcting mechanism is adaptive expectations. This theory asserts that expected inflation and wages partially or gradually adjust to product prices after a time lag of perhaps one year or even longer. The wage adjustment mechanism is slow because of rigidities, bottlenecks, uncertainties, and other inefficiencies associated with wage contracts and negotiations between labor and management. A gradual adjustment occurs as actual unemployment incrementally moves toward natural unemployment. Actual GDP also gradually adjusts toward potential GDP through a partial adjustment mechanism. The economy is often sluggish in moving to long-run equilibrium because of imperfections in market forces.

The Keynesian view maintains that the government should adopt macroeconomic policies to steer the labor market toward full employment and alleviate persistent macroeconomic sluggishness. The Keynesian view and adaptive expectations align with the political left ideology that calls for a relatively large role for the government in the economy to alleviate market failures.

Table 3.3 summarizes the characteristics and differences between the classical and Keynesian viewpoints on the self-correcting mechanism.

Short-Run Effects of Shifts in Macroeconomic Demand and Supply

This section discusses short-run effects of changes in macroeconomic demand and supply on inflation, unemployment, and RGDP. Total macroeconomic demand is the summation of demands for consumption, investment, government purchases, and net exports. An increase in demand for any of the four components of GDP causes a corresponding increase in overall macroeconomic demand.

Higher macroeconomic demand causes product prices to rise. This is called demand-pull inflation. An increase in macroeconomic demand means buyers seek to increase spending and are willing to pay a higher price for products. An increase in the rate of macroeconomic demand

Table 3.3 Classical and Keynesian views on the self-correcting mechanism

Macroeconomic views	Classical perspective	Keynesian perspective
Self-correcting mechanism in the labor market	Relatively fast and efficient adjustment toward full employment	Gradual process of adjustment to full employment
Product market implications	Relatively fast and efficient adjustment toward potential GDP	Gradual process of adjustment toward potential GDP
Adjustment process	In the absence of government policies that distort economic markets, rapid adjustment of expected inflation to actual inflation through a rational-expectations mechanism	Because of market rigidities, gradual adjustment of expected inflation to actual inflation through an adaptive expectations mechanism
Type of inflationary expectations	Rational expectations	Adaptive expectations
Macroeconomic perspective	Classical macroeconomic view	Keynesian macroeconomic view
Ideological perspective	Conservative political view	Liberal political view

causes higher RGDP growth and lower unemployment. Based on Okun's law, lower unemployment occurs as economic growth expands. From a supply-side perspective, business firms employ more workers to produce a greater amount of goods and services to satisfy the higher macroeconomic demand.

A decrease in the rate of demand for consumption, investment, government, or net exports causes a lower rate of aggregate demand. This leads to lower inflation, higher unemployment, and lower RGDP growth. A lower rate of macroeconomic demand means buyers intend to reduce their rate of purchases. Business firms consequently reduce the price rate to induce buyers to purchase goods. Businesses also decrease the production rate because of the reduced rate of demand for goods. Firms therefore hire fewer workers, and the unemployment rate increases.

A shift in macroeconomic supply also has short-run effects on inflation, economic growth, and unemployment. A shift in macroeconomic supply is caused by production-related determinants such as commercial technology, resource productivity, production costs, and government intervention on businesses. For example, cost-saving commercial technology causes an increase in macroeconomic supply. This leads to declining inflation, higher RGDP growth, and lower unemployment. Commercial technology boosts business productivity, which often yields lower production costs. This allows business firms to employ more workers to produce more goods at cheaper prices. Other determinants can also cause lower production costs, such as lower energy expenses. This also leads to an increase in macroeconomic supply, lower inflation, higher real economic growth, and declining unemployment.

Higher production costs, on the other hand, cause a decrease in macroeconomic supply. This leads to higher inflation, lower real economic growth, and worsening unemployment. Higher production costs cause businesses to supply less goods and services. Additionally, higher production costs are partially shifted to buyers in the form of higher product inflation. This is called cost-push inflation. Higher production costs also cause businesses to reduce the production rate to minimize financial losses. Firms consequently hire fewer workers and unemployment worsens because of decreased macroeconomic supply.

A related supply-side factor is expected inflation. This affects worker wages. An increase in expected inflation causes workers to demand higher wages to offset higher expected living expenses. Workers seek higher wages to pay for higher expected prices of goods. The increase in worker wages causes production costs to go up and macroeconomic supply declines. Firms supply less products and hire fewer workers as a cost-cutting measure to counteract higher wage costs. Economic growth declines, unemployment rises, and higher inflation occurs because of higher expected inflation and the decrease in macroeconomic supply.

A decrease in expected inflation creates the opposite effect. Lower expected inflation causes lower wage inflation. Workers accept a lower wage rate because they anticipate a lower rate of product prices. The lower wage rate reduces real production costs. This causes an increase in macroeconomic supply. Firms supply more goods because real production costs go down as real wages decrease. Consequently, economic growth goes up, and unemployment declines. Also, product inflation declines. The lower rate of production costs is passed along to buyers in the form of a lower rate of prices.

Table 3.4 summarizes the short-run macroeconomic supply and demand effects on inflation, unemployment, and real economic growth.

Table 3.4 Short-run macroeconomic demand and supply effects

Short-run macroeconomic effects	Short-run effect on inflation	Short-run effect on RGDP growth	Short-run effect on unemployment
Increase in macroeconomic demand (an increase in demand for consumption, investment, government spending, or net exports)	Higher inflation because buyers wish to purchase more goods and are willing to pay a higher price	Increase in real economic growth because buyers wish to increase spending	Decrease in unemployment because firms hire more workers to increase production to meet the higher demand for goods
Decrease in macroeconomic demand (a decline in demand for consumption, investment, government spending, or net exports)	Decrease in inflation because buyers wish to buy less goods, which forces firms to reduce the rate of product prices	Decrease in real economic growth because buyers wish to reduce their rate of spending	Increase in unemployment because firms hire fewer workers as they reduce production to meet the lower demand for goods
Increase in macroeconomic supply (lower production costs, lower expected inflation, and commercial technology)	Decrease in inflation because lower production costs allow for lower product prices	Increase in real economic growth because firms can produce more goods at lower costs	Decrease in unemployment as firms employ more workers to supply more goods
Decrease in macroeconomic supply (higher production costs and higher expected inflation)	Increase in inflation because higher resource costs are shifted to buyers in the form of higher prices	Decrease in real economic growth because firms cut the rate of production to offset higher resource costs	Increase in unemployment as firms employ fewer workers and supply less goods

Expectational Phillips Curve

The expectations-augmented Phillips curve is also called the expectational Phillips curve. The expectational Phillips curve model expresses macroeconomic supply and demand in terms of inflation and unemployment.[1] This model is named after the late economist William Phillips (1958),

---

[1] See Dornbusch, Fischer, and Startz (2011) for an intermediate level discussion of the expectations-augmented Phillips curve model.

who did research on the empirical correlation between unemployment and wage inflation. The expectational Phillips curve indicates an inverse relation between inflation and unemployment in the short run but not in the long run.[2] The expectations-augmented Phillips curve is relevant to the study of the political macroeconomy because inflation and unemployment are important political considerations. In Chapters 6, 7, and 8, we will examine the political macroeconomic effects of the electoral cycle and the partisan cycle using the expectational Phillips curve.

Figure 3.2 shows the expectational Phillips curve framework.

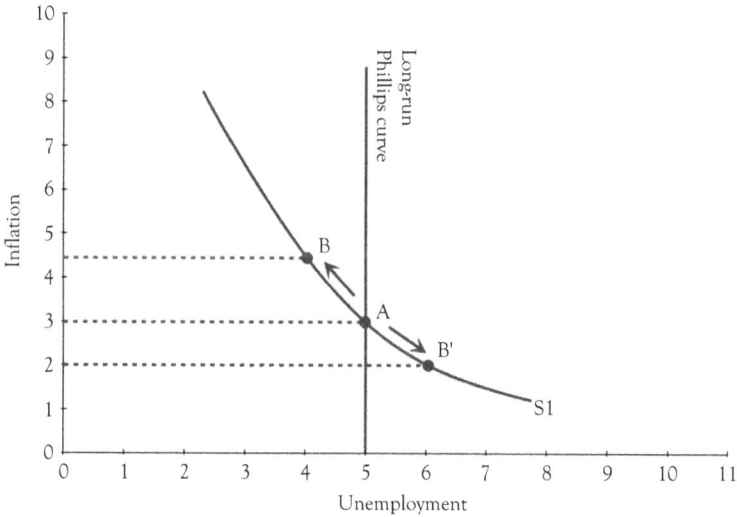

Figure 3.2 Expectational Phillips curve

Inflation is measured along the vertical axis and unemployment is next to the horizontal axis. The vertical line is the long-run Phillips curve. This occurs at the natural rate of unemployment. The downward sloping curve S1 is the short-run Phillips curve. This curve shows short-run macroeconomic supply in terms of unemployment and inflation. The downward slope of the curve is the short-run trade-off between inflation and unemployment. In the short run, an increase in inflation is associated with a decline in unemployment and vice versa. The short-run trade-off

[2]Milton Friedman (1968) emphasized expected inflation plays as a major factor in the relation between inflation and unemployment in the short run and in the long run.

occurs as a movement along the curve S1. A change in the rate of macroeconomic demand causes a movement along the short-run Phillips curve. This affects inflation and unemployment. The movement occurs to the left or right along the curve depending on whether aggregate demand increases or decreases.

A higher rate of macroeconomic demand causes higher demand-pull inflation and a leftward movement along the curve. This is shown as the movement from A to B. Inflation rises and unemployment falls. In contrast, the movement from A to B′ shows falling inflation and rising unemployment. This occurs from a decrease in the rate of macroeconomic demand.

The level of expected inflation corresponds to the intersection between the short-run and long-run Phillips curves. In Figure 3.2, expected inflation is 3 percent. The cross between the short-run and long-run Phillips curves is a long-run equilibrium point. This is shown as point A. If the economy is at point A, then expected inflation and worker wages are aligned with product inflation. The economy is efficient. Expected inflation equals actual inflation of 3 percent. The wage rate is in equilibrium, and the labor market clears at natural unemployment.

A change in expected inflation affects wage inflation and production costs. This causes the curve to shift. The short-run Phillips curve shifts either to the right or the left based on whether expected inflation rises or falls. If expected inflation increases, then worker wages and production costs rise at a faster rate, and the short-run Phillips curve shifts right. If expected inflation declines, then the wage rate goes down, and the short-run Phillips curve shifts leftward.

Short-Run and Long-Run Effects of an Increase in Macroeconomic Demand

Let us consider the effects of an increase in macroeconomic demand in the expectational Phillips curve model. Figure 3.3 shows the results.

Suppose the economy is in long-run equilibrium at point A. Expected inflation and wage inflation are in step with actual inflation at 3 percent. Additionally, unemployment is at the natural rate. Now, assume the rate of macroeconomic demand rises. This is shown as a movement

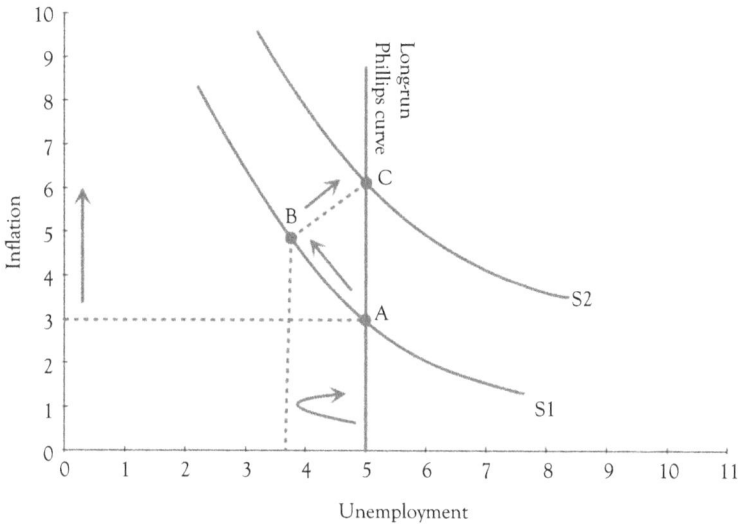

Figure 3.3 Increase in macroeconomic demand

up and to the left along the short-run Phillips curve from long-run point A to the short-run outcome at point B. This assumes expected inflation is unchanged at 3 percent. This movement along the curve causes lower unemployment and higher inflation. Product inflation rises from 3 to about 5 percent, while unemployment declines from the natural rate of 5 percent to around 3.67 percent. Point B is a short-run outcome because unemployment is less than the natural rate.

For example, the higher rate of aggregate demand could occur from expansionary monetary policy that is intended to reduce unemployment and increase RGDP growth. Inflation, however, worsens as a side effect of the higher rate of macroeconomic demand. A higher rate of macroeconomic demand means that consumers and businesses increase spending. This drives up prices and causes rising inflation. Additionally, the higher rate of spending requires more production and labor. This causes unemployment to fall.

At point B, unexpected inflation is 2 percent (2 = actual inflation − expected inflation = 5 − 3). Prices rise faster than anticipated. Producers sell goods at higher prices than originally planned. Actual inflation rises to around 5 percent, while expected inflation and the wage rate stay at 3 percent. Unemployment, correspondingly, declines from the natural rate of 5 percent to around 3.67 percent. Firms produce more goods and hire more workers because higher-than-expected prices yield greater opportunities for sales and profits.

In the long run, macroeconomic supply declines. Lower macroeconomic supply occurs through the self-correcting mechanism in reaction to higher macroeconomic demand. The short-run Philips curve shifts right from S1 to S2. This occurs as workers increase their inflationary expectations in response to higher actual inflation. Workers demand higher wages to offset higher product prices. Expected inflation and the wage rate rise and adjust to actual inflation through the self-correcting mechanism. Firms then shift the higher labor costs to buyers in the form of higher product prices. This leads to a further inflationary increase. Business firms also reduce the number of workers employed to partially offset the higher labor costs.

The economy moves from short-run point B to long-run equilibrium at point C through the self-correcting mechanism. This corresponds to the rightward shift of the short-run Phillips curve from S1 to S2. Inflation rises further from 5 to 6 percent, while unemployment adjusts from 3.67 percent back to natural unemployment at the new long-run equilibrium at point C.

In summary, higher macroeconomic demand causes a movement to the left along the short-run Phillips curve. This is followed by a rightward shift of the curve because of the self-correcting mechanism. This creates macroeconomic overheating or rising demand-pull inflation. If the economy is initially at potential, then an increase in macroeconomic demand causes only a temporary improvement in unemployment along with the side effect of higher inflation.

Short-Run and Long-Run Effects of a Decrease in Macroeconomic Demand

Consider the short and long-run effects of a decline in macroeconomic demand in the expectational Phillips curve framework. Figure 3.4 shows the results.

Suppose the economy is in long-run equilibrium at point C. Both actual and expected inflation are relatively high at about 6 percent. Now, assume macroeconomic demand declines, perhaps from contractionary monetary policy designed to reduce inflation. The economy moves down

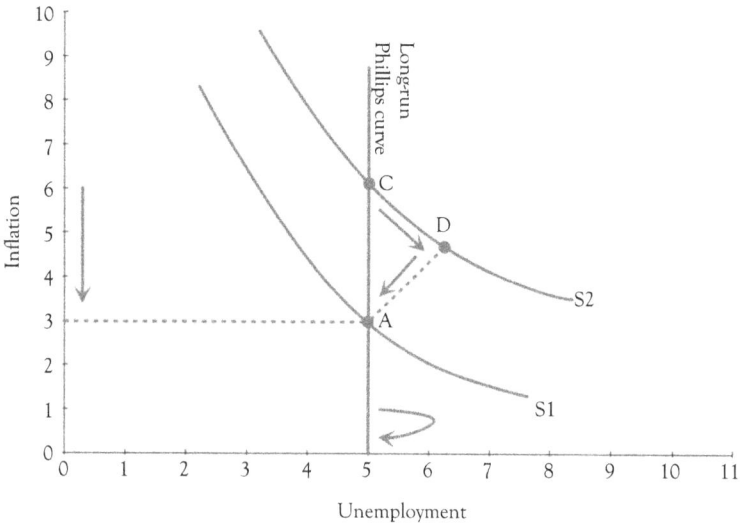

Figure 3.4 Decrease in macroeconomic demand

and to the right along the short-run Phillips curve S2 from long-run point C to short-run point D. The decrease in macroeconomic demand is associated with less spending on goods and services, less production, less employment, reduced economic growth, and lower inflation.

Inflation falls from 6 to about 5 percent, while expected inflation and the wage rate stay at 6 percent in the short run. This creates negative unexpected inflation of −1 percent (= 5 − 6). Prices end up lower than originally expected. Because of the decreased macroeconomic demand, producers must sell products at a lower price than initially anticipated to induce consumers to purchase products. Firms receive less revenues and profits than originally planned. Businesses consequently reduce production as a cost-cutting devise. Firms employ fewer workers, and unemployment rises above the natural rate from 5 to 6 percent at short-run point D. Firms reduce production to meet the reduced rate of demand in the economy. Since these results occur in the short run, we assume production costs are constant, including labor wages and expected inflation.

In the long run, the economy moves back to equilibrium at natural unemployment through the self-correcting mechanism. The short-run Phillips curve shifts left from S2 to S1, and the economy adjusts from point D to point A. Firms reduce the wage rate to minimize the adverse effect of lost revenues. Workers, correspondingly, are willing to accept the lower wage rate because lower inflation makes products more affordable.

The lower wage rate causes the rate of production costs to decrease. This supply-side effect allows businesses to raise output and rehire workers. Business firms respond to the lower rate of resource costs by producing more goods to earn more revenues and profits. The lower rate of production costs also permits a further decline in product inflation. The lower rate of production costs enables firms to sell products at a lower price rate. The economy consequently moves back to long-run equilibrium at the natural unemployment rate at point A.

In summary, a short-run disinflationary economic contraction occurs from a decline in aggregate demand. The decline in macroeconomic demand causes unemployment to temporarily worsen while inflation falls in both the short run and long run.

Business Cycle Pattern in the Phillips Curve Framework

Figure 3.5 shows the overall spiral pattern of the business cycle in terms of unemployment and inflation. This is shown in the expectational Phillips curve framework. The diagram combines the effects of Figure 3.3 and Figure 3.4.

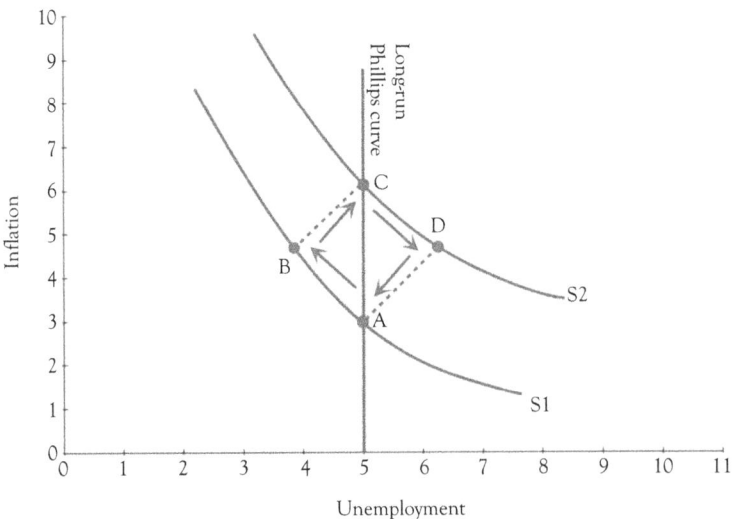

Figure 3.5 Business cycle in terms of inflation and unemployment

Assume the economy is in long-run equilibrium at natural unemployment at point A. Now suppose an increase in macroeconomic demand occurs. Let us suppose this occurs from an expansionary monetary policy intended to reduce unemployment. The economy moves along the short-run Phillips curve S1 from point A to point B. The economy is now in short-run disequilibrium. The self-correcting mechanism of market forces consequently comes into play. The short-run Phillips curve shifts to the right from S1 to S2. This occurs as expected inflation and wage inflation rise to adjust to the increase in actual inflation. The economy moves from point B to long-run equilibrium at the natural unemployment rate at point C.

Next, assume a decrease in macroeconomic demand occurs. Let us suppose this occurs from a contractionary monetary policy designed to reduce inflation. The economy moves from long-run point C to short-run point D along the short-run Phillips curve S2. Inflation falls while unemployment worsens. The economy is in disequilibrium. At short-run point D, the self-correcting mechanism of market forces causes the economy to adjust back to natural unemployment. The short-run Phillips curve shifts left from S2 to S1 as employers reduce the wage rate in response to the decrease in expected inflation. Expected inflation falls and adjusts to decline in actual inflation. The economy moves to point A in long-run equilibrium at the natural unemployment rate.

A clockwise business cycle pattern takes place as the economy moves from point A to point B to point C to point D and finally back to point A. In the actual economy, however, inflation and unemployment do not always exhibit this idealized pattern. Economic rigidities, imperfections, unexpected economic shocks, and uncertainties can cause the economy to deviate somewhat from the model. Figure 3.6 shows a sample of the U.S. business cycle. The highlighted years in the chart correspond to presidential elections.

The chart shows the dynamics of unemployment and inflation in the U.S. economy over the period from 1961 to 1984. The outcomes do not perfectly match the symmetrical clockwise result in Figure 3.5. The pattern of inflation and unemployment, however, shows a general clockwise effect.

Consumer price index for all urban consumers: All items (CPIAUCSL)
civilian unemployment rate (UNRATE)

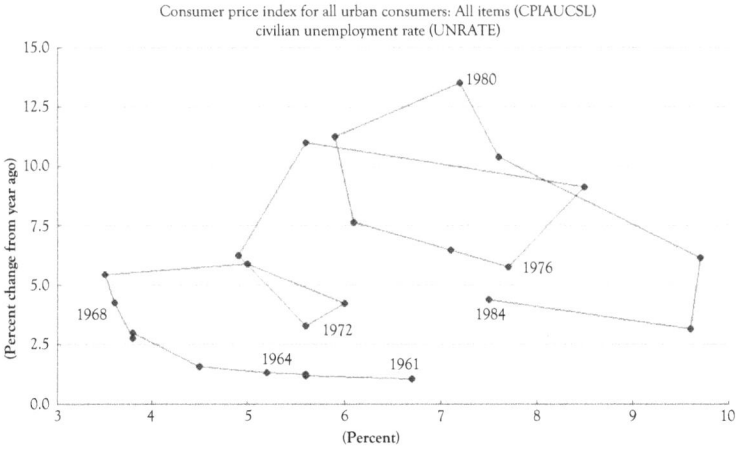

Figure 3.6 U.S. business cycle pattern

Source: Federal Reserve Economic Data (FRED)

Resolving a Recession: The Classical View versus the Keynesian View

Two opposing viewpoints occur on the role of government activism versus market forces in the macroeconomy. The two perspectives are the classical view and the Keynesian view. The two perspectives advocate differing approaches for resolving a recession.

The classical outlook advocates a small role for government in the economy and a large role for market forces. According to the classical perspective, a small government allows a larger and more efficient private sector to flourish. The political right typically embraces the classical macroeconomic viewpoint. The Keynesian outlook advocates a stronger role for government in the macroeconomy, especially if a long-lasting or severe recession occurs. The political left generally adopts the Keynesian perspective. The political left usually advocates a more activist macroeconomic policy.

Figure 3.7 contrasts Keynesianism versus classicalism on resolving a recession in the expectational Phillips curve framework.

Suppose the economy is in a recessionary gap at point 1. Unemployment is about 6 percent, which is greater than the natural rate of 5 percent. Product inflation is about 4½ percent and expected inflation is

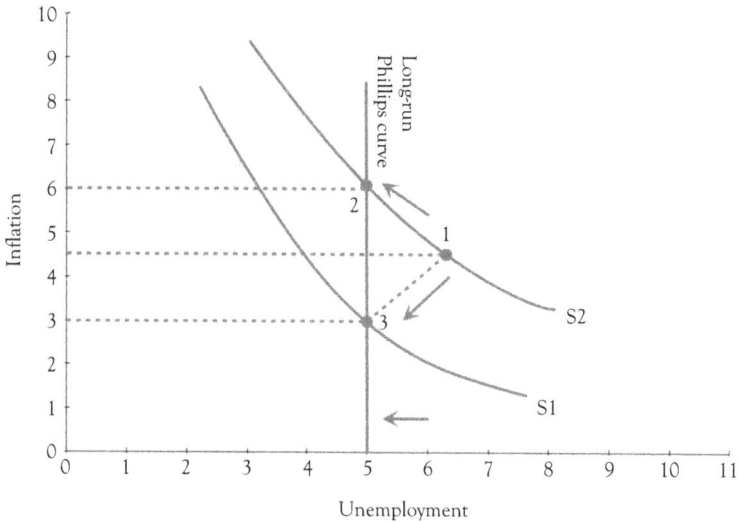

Figure 3.7 Two approaches for resolving a recessionary gap

6 percent. Expected inflation of 6 percent corresponds to the cross between the vertical long-run Phillips curve and the short-run Phillips curve S2.

The Keynesian approach to a recessionary gap consists of activist macroeconomic policy, such as expansionary monetary policy. Through expansionary policy, aggregate demand rises. The economy consequently moves to the left along the short-run Phillips curve S2 from point 1 to long-run equilibrium at point 2. The increase in macroeconomic demand facilitates greater purchases of goods and services, as well as greater employment to produce more goods.

The expansionary policy alleviates the recessionary gap. This policy, however, has a trade-off of higher inflation. Higher macroeconomic demand means buyers increase expenditures and are willing to pay higher prices for products. Inflation rises from 4½ to 6 percent as the economy moves from point 1 to point 2. This negative side effect of higher inflation is a major drawback of expansionary policy according to the classical view.

The classical perspective maintains that the self-correcting mechanism of market forces is often a superior approach to resolving a recession, especially if the recession is mild. The self-correcting mechanism consists of the adjustment of expected inflation and wage inflation to actual inflation through the natural process of market forces. At point 1, expected inflation is 6 percent, which is more than actual inflation of 4½ percent. Negative unexpected inflation of $-1½$ percent occurs $(-1½ = 4½ - 6)$. Employees and employers consequently reduce inflationary expectations to coincide with actual inflation, and the wage rate declines. The rate of production costs therefore decreases, and the short-run Phillips curve shifts left from S2 to S1.

Businesses reduce the worker wage rate as a cost-cutting devise because product prices are lower than anticipated. In the long run, as the wage rate falls, businesses rehire laid-off workers. Through this self-correcting mechanism, the economy improves and settles in long-run equilibrium at point 3. Unemployment declines from 6 percent to the natural rate of 5 percent, alleviating the recessionary gap. Additionally, inflation falls from 4½ to 3 percent because of the decline in the wage rate. The lower wage rate enables businesses to reduce the rate of product prices. An advantage of the classical approach for curing a recession, assuming the self-correcting mechanism works efficiently, is that both inflation and unemployment decrease simultaneously.

A criticism of the classical approach from the Keynesian viewpoint is that the self-correcting mechanism is often slow. The automatic adjustment of the economy from point 1 to point 3 may require a long period of time. Keynesianism maintains that expansionary macroeconomic policy can alleviate a severe recession more effectively and faster than the natural process of the self-correcting mechanism.

Impact of Energy Prices on the Macroeconomy

Let us consider the influence of energy prices (such as fossil fuels) on the economy using the expectational Phillips curve. This issue has historically been important for the United States. In the past, the United States has imported a substantial amount of oil, particularly from the OPEC cartel. The impact of oil prices on the U.S. economy has at times been considerable, particularly during the two oil shocks of the 1970s. This decade of oil crises was followed by a decline in oil prices throughout much of the 1980s, with notable up-and-down price fluctuations since then.

Oil is a primary energy source for the U.S. economy and has an important effect on macroeconomic supply. The cost of oil is a macroeconomic supply-side determinant because of the impact on production costs. If oil and gas prices rise, especially a dramatic increase, then stagflation could develop. Stagflation is the simultaneous increase of both inflation and unemployment. If energy costs rise, then macroeconomic supply declines and inflation and unemployment worsen. This is shown in Figure 3.8.

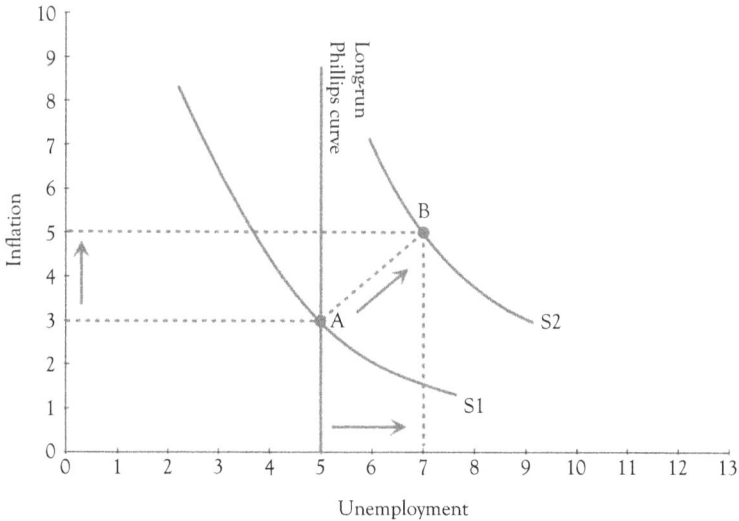

Figure 3.8 Short-run effects of a substantial increase in the price of oil

Suppose the economy is at point A in long-run equilibrium at natural unemployment. A large increase in the price of oil causes lower macroeconomic supply and the short-run Phillips curve shifts right from S1 to S2. The economy moves from point A to point B. Product inflation rises from 3 to 5 percent as higher energy costs are shifted to consumers as higher product prices. Meanwhile, unemployment rises from 5 to 7 percent as firms reduce production and employment as a cost-cutting tactic to minimize the impact of higher energy prices on production expenses.

Now consider the reverse result of a major decrease in oil prices. If oil prices decline substantially (perhaps from the modern mining technique of hydraulic fracturing or fracking), then lower inflation and lower unemployment may occur. This is shown in Figure 3.9.

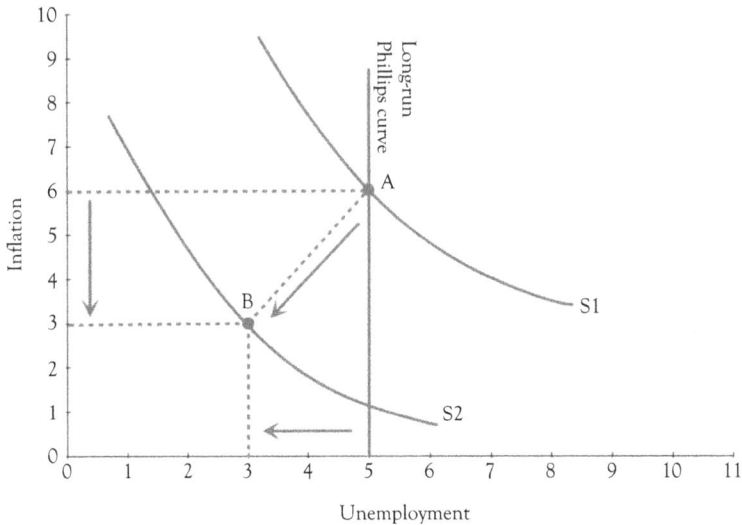

Figure 3.9 Short-run effects of a substantial decrease in the price of oil

Suppose the economy is at point A in long-run equilibrium at natural unemployment. Next, assume oil prices decrease. This causes an expansion in macroeconomic supply and the short-run Phillips curve shifts left from S1 to S2. The economy moves from long-run point A to short-run point B. Business firms respond to lower oil prices by raising production and lowering the rate of product prices. Inflation declines from 6 to 3 percent as the effect of lower energy costs are transferred to consumers as lower prices. Additionally, unemployment falls from 5 to 3 percent. Lower oil prices allow production costs to fall, which makes hiring additional labor more affordable.

Oil prices have fluctuated up and down over time. The overall trend, however, has been a rise in oil prices with variations. Figure 3.10 shows the pattern of oil prices since the mid-1940s.

The price of crude oil was $3.50 per barrel or less from the mid-1940s to the early 1970s. Oil prices then spiked upward twice during the mid- and late-1970s. The first oil shock was in 1973, and the second was in 1979. Both oil shocks negatively impacted the U.S. economy. Stagflation occurred, consisting of rising inflation and worsening unemployment. This arose from a decrease in macroeconomic supply due to high oil prices. During the 1980s and 1990s, oil prices tended to decline. Since the year 2000, oil prices have risen but with fluctuations.

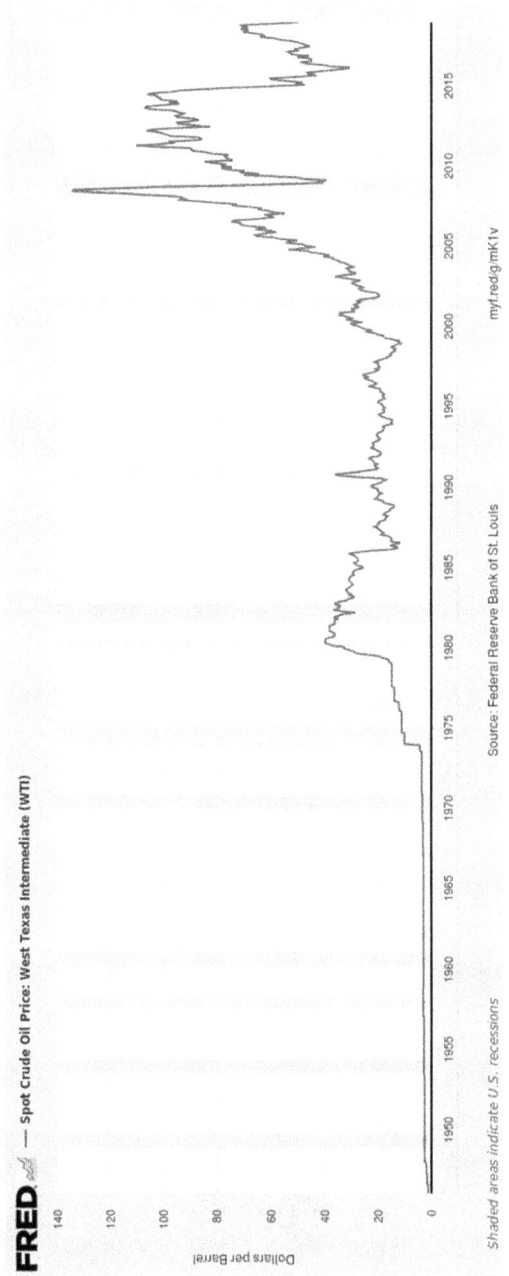

Figure 3.10 Crude oil prices, 1946–2018

Source: FRED

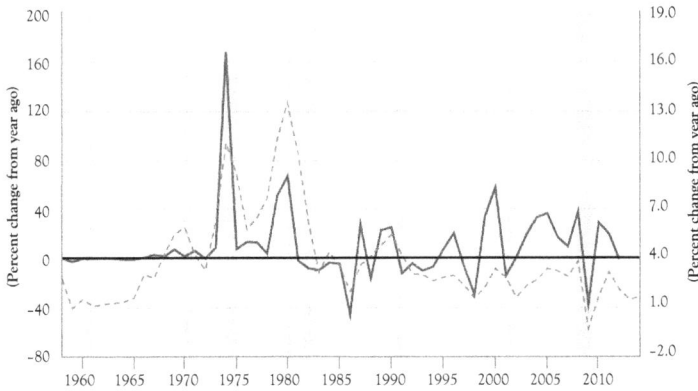

Figure 3.11 Relation between oil prices and inflation

Source: FRED

Oil prices affect overall inflation, as depicted in Figures 3.8 and 3.9. The empirical correlation between actual oil prices and overall inflation is shown in Figure 3.11. The percentage change in the price of oil is measured along the left vertical axis and overall price inflation is measured next to the right vertical axis. Oil price inflation is shown as the solid line. General price inflation is shown as the dashed line. A positive correlation occurs between oil price inflation and overall inflation. During time periods when oil prices rose dramatically, general inflation also tended to rise. This is particularly evident during the two energy crises of 1973 and 1979. In both instances, stagflation arose. The oil shocks led to high inflation as well as recessions. The vertical shaded areas in the chart denote economic recessions. On the other hand, when oil prices fell, overall inflation went down. For example, declining inflation occurred alongside decreasing oil prices throughout the first half of the 1980s. This contrasts with high oil prices and high inflation during the oil shocks of the 1970s.

The issue of oil prices has political macroeconomy ramifications because of the impact on inflation and unemployment, especially during the Nixon–Ford, Carter, and Reagan presidencies. Chapter 8 examines the impact of oil prices on political macroeconomic effects during those administrations.

CHAPTER 4

Fiscal and Monetary Policies

Introduction: Expansionary and Contractionary Policies

The macroeconomic policymakers are the president, Congress, and the Federal Reserve. Macroeconomic policies are also referred to as stabilization policies. The government adopts macroeconomic policies to improve and stabilize economic performance. Stabilization policies focus on macroeconomic goals such as high real GDP growth, low unemployment, and low stable inflation. To attain these objectives, macroeconomic policies may be expansionary or contractionary.

Expansionary policies are used to alleviate a macroeconomic slowdown, in other words a recessionary gap. Keynesianism is the active use of an expansionary policy to cure a weak economy. According to Keynesianism, an expansionary policy increases aggregate demand, which increases economic growth and reduces unemployment. Keynesianism contrasts with the classical view for resolving a recessionary gap. Classicalism emphasizes the process of market forces rather than government activism.

Figure 4.1 shows the impact of a Keynesian expansionary policy in the expectational Phillips curve framework.

Suppose the economy is at point 1 in a recessionary gap. Unemployment is equal to 6 percent. This is greater than the natural rate of 5 percent. Inflation is about 2 percent at point 1. Now, assume the government seeks to close the recessionary gap through an expansionary macroeconomic policy. Macroeconomic demand rises. This leads to higher RGDP growth and lower unemployment. The economy moves up and to the left along the short-run Phillips curve S1 from point 1 to point 2. The recessionary gap is resolved as unemployment declines from 6 percent to the natural rate of 5 percent. An expansionary policy, however, may cause an adverse side effect of higher inflation. Demand-pull inflation develops as

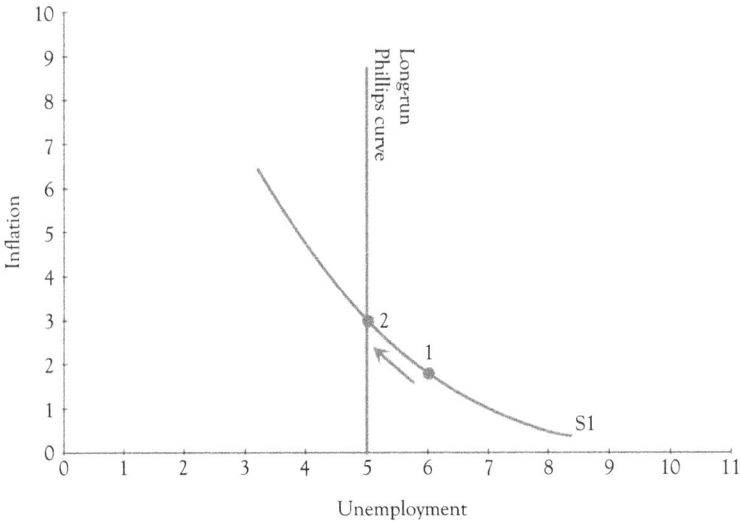

Figure 4.1 Expansionary macroeconomic policy

businesses and households increase demand for spending and are willing to pay higher prices. Inflation rises from 2 to 3 percent as the economy moves from point 1 to point 2. Given the initial recessionary gap, the effects of an expansionary policy are lower unemployment and higher inflation.

A contractionary macroeconomic policy decreases aggregate demand to alleviate an inflationary gap. The goal of contractionary policy is to reduce inflation. Figure 4.2 shows the effects of a contractionary policy in the expectational Phillips curve model.

Assume the economy is at point A. Unemployment is about 4 percent. This is less than the natural unemployment rate of 5 percent. The economy is in an inflationary gap and overheated. Excess macroeconomic demand occurs. Excess macroeconomic demand causes rising inflation. Inflation is about 4.5 percent at point A. Inflation is likely to rise further if excess macroeconomic demand persists.

Suppose the policymakers seek to resolve the excess macroeconomic demand or inflationary gap through a contractionary policy. Macroeconomic demand decreases. The economy moves down and to the right along the short-run Phillips curve S1 from point A to point B. The inflationary gap is closed by decreasing macroeconomic demand. Inflation

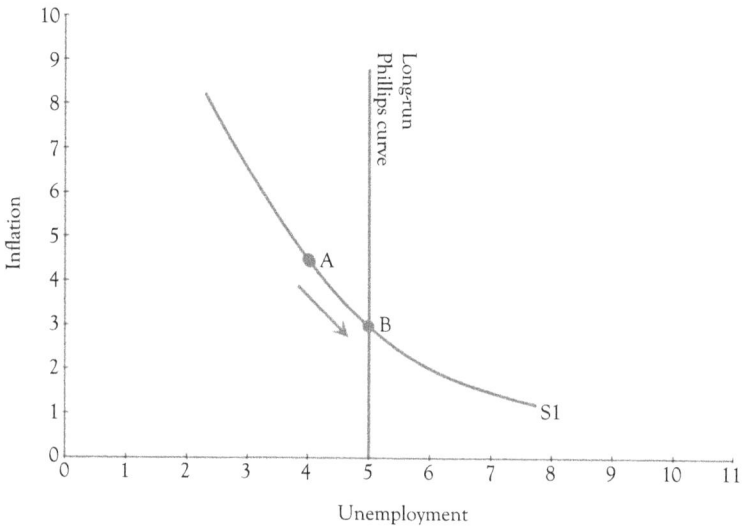

Figure 4.2 Contractionary macroeconomic policy

falls from 4.5 to 3 percent. The contractionary policy also causes un-employment to rise from 4 percent to the natural rate of 5 percent. The contractionary policy alleviates macroeconomic overheating, and the economy moves to a long-run position of efficiency at point B. This point is efficient because it occurs on the long-run Phillips curve.

Fiscal Policy: Government Spending and Taxes

Two kinds of macroeconomic policies are available for expansionary and contractionary purposes. They are fiscal policy and monetary policy. Fiscal policy is the influence of government expenditures and taxes on mac-roeconomic demand and the economy as typically measured by RGDP, unemployment, inflation, and interest rates. Some of the main types of government taxes are personal and corporate income taxes, social secu-rity taxes, sales taxes, property taxes, and excise taxes. Some of the main types of government spending are national defense, government-provided health care such as Medicare and Medicaid, and public education.

The government budget equals total government spending minus total taxes. A government budget deficit occurs if government spending exceeds total taxes. A budget surplus arises if total government spending is less than total taxes. A balanced budget takes place if total government spending equals total taxes. Government debt is approximately equal to the sum of all past and present government deficits and surpluses. A government deficit causes government debt to increase, while a government surplus causes government debt to decline.

The government finances its debt obligations by borrowing from the public through issuing treasury bonds. The public consists of individuals, businesses, private banks, the central bank, and foreign buyers including foreign governments. The treasury borrows funds by printing treasury bonds that are sold to the public. From the public's perspective, the purchase of treasury bonds is a financial investment that earns interest. From the government's point of view, treasury bonds are the means by which the government borrows funds to finance budget deficits. A sizable portion of the national debt is purchased and held as an asset in the balance sheet of the central bank. The central bank buys treasury bonds from the public by printing new currency. This causes money supply in the economy to expand. This relates to the money supply process that is discussed later in this chapter.

Expansionary Fiscal Policy: Higher Government Spending and Lower Taxes

Fiscal policy may be expansionary or contractionary, based on whether unemployment or inflation is considered the main economic concern by policymakers. An expansionary fiscal policy focuses on attaining higher economic growth and lower unemployment. An expansionary fiscal policy consists of two tools, which are tax cuts and higher government spending.

The first tool is lower taxes. Lower income taxes among households and businesses create higher after-tax income for businesses and households. After-tax household income is called disposable income. Higher disposable income enables more consumer spending. Higher after-tax business income, such as after-tax retained corporate earnings, enables more business spending on investment in plant and equipment. Tax cuts indirectly facilitate greater consumption and investment spending among households and businesses. Lower taxes lead to higher after-tax income, greater spending, and higher aggregate demand.

The other expansionary fiscal policy tool, besides tax cuts, is higher government spending. Higher government spending directly increases macroeconomic demand. This is because government expenditure is a direct component of GDP. For example, the initial effect of higher government spending of $100 billion is an increase in GDP of $100 billion. We will discuss the subsequent effects of higher government spending later in this chapter, such as crowding-in, crowding-out, and the spending multiplier.

An expansionary fiscal policy expands macroeconomic demand. This increases RGDP and reduces unemployment. An expansionary policy, however, may cause a negative side effect of worsening inflation. The effect of an expansionary fiscal policy is shown as the movement from point 1 to point 2 in Figure 4.1. Fiscal policy also affects the government budget deficit and national debt. An expansionary fiscal policy of greater government spending or lower taxes causes a larger government budget deficit and higher national debt.

The classical macroeconomic perspective and the political right generally advocate lower taxes as the preferable expansionary fiscal policy. Lower taxes reduce the role and size of government in the economy. This permits a greater role for market forces in the economy. The classical outlook view market forces as more effective and efficient than government spending.

The Keynesian outlook and the political left often advise higher government spending as an effective expansionary fiscal policy. According to Keynesianism, higher government expenditures can offset economic slowdown in the private sector. If the private sector is weak, government spending may be increased to counterbalance low consumer spending and low business spending. Keynesianism asserts that market forces are sometimes insufficient to create a strong economy.

For an expansionary fiscal policy, Keynesianism often advocates higher government spending. This has a stronger, quicker, more reliable, and more direct impact on the economy than tax cuts. Lower taxes directly increase after-tax income. This, however, has an indirect and less certain impact on spending. Tax cuts, for example, could cause more household or business saving rather than more spending.

For instance, rather than increasing business spending, lower corporate taxes could induce corporations to buy back stocks to increase the stock price and increase shareholder wealth. If saving rises instead of spending from a tax cut, then the impact on macroeconomic demand is limited. Spending is the driving force on macroeconomic demand. The higher the spending, the higher the macroeconomic demand.

Government spending has an immediate and direct impact on macroeconomic demand and GDP. This is because government spending is a direct component of GDP. Keynesianism generally advocates higher government spending as an effective expansionary policy to create stronger economic growth. Higher government spending is a direct approach to offset weak private sector spending. Classicalism, on the other hand, generally embraces lower taxes as an effective expansionary policy to enhance economic growth. A tax cut shrinks the role of government and boosts the private sector of the economy.

Crowding-out and Crowding-in Effects

The crowding-out effect and the crowding-in effect are two important influences regarding the effectiveness of an expansionary fiscal policy. The crowding-out effect is a major factor in an efficient full-employment economy. The crowding-in effect is a major factor in an inefficient economy, such as a recession. The stronger the economy, the larger the crowding-out effect and the smaller the crowding-in effect. The weaker the economy, the smaller the crowding-out effect and the larger the crowding-in effect.

The classical view emphasizes the crowding-out effect. The crowding-out effect refers to the harmful impact that may occur from government deficit spending in a full-employment economy. The Keynesian perspective emphasizes the crowding-in effect. The crowding-in effect refers to the positive impact that may occur from government deficit spending in a weak economy.

Crowding-out is the adverse impact of government deficit spending on interest rates and business investment. Higher government spending causes the government deficit to worsen, assuming taxes are constant.

A higher budget deficit may cause higher interest rates. This occurs because higher government borrowing to finance a budget deficit competes with private sector borrowing by businesses and households. The overall demand for borrowing throughout the economy increases when government debt rises. The total demand for borrowing is called the demand for loanable funds. This equals government borrowing plus private sector borrowing.

An increase in the demand for loanable funds caused by higher government debt may bid up the cost of borrowing. The interest rate is the cost of borrowing. Higher government spending and a higher budget deficit may cause higher interest rates. If interest rates rise, business borrowing to finance investment in plant and equipment becomes more expensive. Business firms consequently reduce borrowing to fund capital investment. Business investment declines and is crowded out because of higher interest rates associated with higher government debt.

If complete crowding-out occurs, then higher government spending and higher budget deficits are completely negated by an equal decline in private investment spending. Business investment declines as government spending rises. This leaves Real GDP essentially unchanged, but with higher interest rates and greater government debt. As business investment declines, future economic growth may similarly decrease.

Crowding-out, however, is likely to be partial rather than full. Government deficit spending and higher debt may cause lower private economic investment. The two effects, however, may not completely cancel out. An increase in government deficit spending by $100 billion, for example, may cause interest rates to rise and private investment to fall by $25 billion rather than $100 billion. This is partial crowding-out.

Lower government deficit spending, on the other hand, may enable greater business investment spending. A smaller government deficit reduces the demand for loanable funds. This may cause lower interest rates. If interest rates drop, business firms may increase borrowing to finance new investment in plant and equipment.

Crowding-out is likely to happen if the economy is at or near potential or full capacity. The crowding-in effect, by comparison, occurs when the economy is in a recession or experiencing low growth. Crowding-in takes place if government deficit spending triggers an even greater expansion in macroeconomic demand through the spending multiplier. According to the crowding-in effect or the spending multiplier effect, higher government expenditure triggers increases in consumer spending and higher GDP.

Suppose government spending rises by $100 billion. GDP consequently rises by $100 billion because government purchases are a direct part of GDP. This increase in government spending generates higher income of $100 billion to the sellers or suppliers of government products. For example, the suppliers could be health care providers in the Medicare program or government contractors that supply military equipment for national defense.

The suppliers of government goods spend a portion of their $100 billion in new income, perhaps $75 billion on consumer goods. This second round of spending causes GDP to rise by an additional $75 billion. This creates a further round of income, this time to sellers of consumer goods. They, in turn, increase their spending, perhaps by $60 billion. This leads to yet another round of new income and subsequent spending.

Through this multiplier process, higher government spending creates an even greater impact on macroeconomic demand and GDP. Essentially, one person's spending becomes someone else's income. This leads to more spending and income to others. This ripple effect of multiple rounds of income and spending occurs in response to the initial rise in government purchases. If overall macroeconomic demand eventually expands by $250 billion in reaction to an initial increase in government purchases of $100 billion, then the spending multiplier is 2.5.

Keynesianism emphasizes the crowding-in effect or spending multiplier effect of government purchases, including deficit spending, upon GDP. The classical perspective emphasizes the crowding-out effect of increased government deficit spending on higher interest rates and the possibility of reduced business investment.

Contractionary Fiscal Policy: Lower Government Spending and Higher Taxes

Government spending and taxes may be used for a contractionary macroeconomic policy. A contractionary fiscal policy may occur in two ways.

They are higher taxes or lower government spending. The main goal of a contractionary fiscal policy is to reduce inflationary pressures by lowering macroeconomic demand. This, however, may cause a side effect of lower economic growth and higher unemployment. This occurs because of the short-run inflation-unemployment trade-off. A contractionary policy causes lower inflation but also less spending in the economy and fewer jobs.

A side effect of a contractionary fiscal policy is that the government budget deficit may decline. Higher taxes or lower government spending cause the budget deficit to decrease. Additionally, national debt may decline if a budget surplus occurs from higher taxes or lower government purchases.

The first type of contractionary fiscal policy is higher taxes. An increase in taxes indirectly causes lower spending. This takes place through the intermediate impact of higher taxes on after-tax household and business income. Higher taxes cause after-tax income to fall for households and businesses. Less funds are available for business investment and household consumption because of higher taxes. Lower after-tax income induces businesses and households to reduce spending. Macroeconomic demand accordingly declines. Besides higher taxes, the other contractionary fiscal policy is lower government purchases. Lower government expenditure directly decreases aggregate demand and GDP because government spending is a direct part of GDP.

Classical View and the Political Right on Contractionary Fiscal Policy

The classical perspective on contractionary fiscal policy normally prescribes lower government spending rather than higher taxes to manage inflation. Lower government expenditure reduces the role and size of the state in the economy. This is a major priority of the classical view and the political right. The political right tends to adhere to the classical macroeconomic perspective that advocates a small government sector and a large private sector.

The political right also generally advocates lower spending on government social programs rather than cuts in national defense for contractionary fiscal policy. Two considerations underlie this conservative preference on government spending. They are economic self-reliance and strong national security.

The political right stresses that the long-term solution to poverty is individual economic self-sufficiency through employment for those who are able to work. Employment is the means to self-reliance in a capitalist society. The political right maintains that government subsidies and programs that address poverty can become counterproductive. Government spending to help the poor can inadvertently perpetuate economic dependency. Government programs that deal with poverty may prolong poverty. Some recipients of government assistance may perpetually rely on government aid. The political right and the classical economic view assert that lower social spending compels some long-term recipients of government aid to seek employment.

The political left, on the other hand, maintain that cuts in antipoverty programs worsen poverty among the poor and disabled who fall between the cracks of the market system. Lower social spending causes some long-term welfare recipients to seek work. Those who do not obtain employment, however, find that their poverty worsens because of reduced social spending.

The second conservative principle on contractionary fiscal policy is the concept of strong national security. The 19th century economic philosopher Adam Smith is often considered the father of modern economics. Smith wrote on the role of the state in society and the economy. One of the main functions of government is a strong national defense according to Adam Smith and many others. Strong national security promotes a safe, secure, and stable social and economic environment for the private sector to thrive. High military spending enhances national security according to the political right. Political conservatism tends to adopt a hawkish sentiment on national security. The best way to prevent war is to prepare for war through strong national defense. The political right consequently tends to oppose military spending cuts as a contractionary fiscal policy.

Keynesian View on Contractionary Policy

Keynesianism advocates lower government spending as a contractionary fiscal policy to control inflation. The rationale is that government expenditures have a larger, more direct, quicker, and more reliable impact on macroeconomic demand than tax policy. Lower government spending causes an immediate and direct decline in macroeconomic demand.

Taxes, on the other hand, indirectly affect aggregate demand and GDP through the intermediate impact of after-tax income. Taxes directly influence after-tax business and household income. Higher taxes cause lower after-tax income. Lower after-tax business and household income may lead to lower consumption and business spending. However, some economic uncertainty occurs. Some after-tax income goes to saving instead of spending. Higher taxes may have less impact on spending and macroeconomic demand than anticipated because of saving. Households and businesses may react to higher taxes by saving less rather than spending less. If this occurs, macroeconomic demand is unchanged. In this case, consumer and business spending stay the same, while saving decreases because of higher taxes.

The Political Left and Contractionary Fiscal Policy

The political left tends to oppose contractionary fiscal policies of government spending cuts in social safety-net programs such as Medicaid, Medicare, unemployment insurance, social security, and social welfare. The political left emphasizes that lower social spending worsens economic distress among the poor.

Antipoverty government programs are often designed to provide temporary economic relief to low-income households. Social safety-net programs provide economic necessities that otherwise may be unavailable for many of the poor. Government social programs, however, have not been particularly effective in resolving the long-term root causes of poverty. Antipoverty programs can perpetuate poverty if the recipients continually rely on government assistance.

The political left typically opposes cuts in social safety-net programs as a contractionary policy. The political left often advocates lower military spending as a contractionary fiscal policy. The political left tends to embrace a military dove sentiment. Countries that overprepare for war are more likely to go to war. Excess military superiority may create an overconfidence to engage in unnecessary armed conflicts.

The political left also tends to favor a contractionary fiscal policy of higher taxes on the wealthy. The political left often supports a higher marginal income tax rate on higher-income households and businesses. This creates greater equity in disposable income across the socioeconomic spectrum. The marginal income tax rate, according to the political left, should be higher on upper-income households and businesses based on the ability-to-pay principle. Tax rates should be smaller on lower-income individuals and businesses because of lesser ability to pay.

In summary, Keynesianism and the political left generally support higher progressivity of income taxes and cuts in military spending as desirable contractionary fiscal policies to assuage inflationary pressures. The classical macroeconomic view and the political right generally favor lower government spending on social programs as a contractionary fiscal policy to dampen inflation.

The economic and political characteristics of expansionary and contractionary fiscal policies are summarized in Table 4.1.

Table 4.1 Expansionary and contractionary fiscal policies

Fiscal policy	Goals	Possible macroeconomic side effects	Policy tools	Political left	Political right
Expansionary fiscal policy	Remedy recession or sluggish economic growth, reduce unemployment	Higher inflation; larger government budget deficit	Increase in government spending or decrease in taxes	Increase in government spending, especially social programs	Decrease in taxes
Contractionary fiscal policy	Remedy high inflation or economic overheating	Lower economic growth, higher unemployment, possibly recession; smaller government budget deficit	Decrease in government spending or increase in taxes	Increase in progressivity of taxes or reduction in military spending	Decrease in government spending on social programs

The political right and the political left differ on the most effective approach to fiscal policy. This ideological divide is based on opposing views on the role and effectiveness of market forces versus government activism in building a strong economy with low inflation. The political left tends to support Keynesianism, while the political right tends to adhere to classicalism.

Political Influences on the Fiscal Policy Process

Fiscal policy mainly occurs through the federal budget process. This consists of the political interaction and compromise between the president and the Congress. The Congress and the president are the fiscal policymakers. The budget process also involves the macroeconomic agendas of left and right political parties. Most members of Congress and the president belong to one of the two major parties. The interaction between the Congress, the president, and the two main parties in determining fiscal policy may be cooperative or conflictual. The distribution of political party control over the executive and legislative branches affects whether the fiscal policy process is cooperative or conflictual.

If one political party controls both the legislative and executive branches, then the in-party to the White House has a strong likelihood to attain the desired fiscal policy. The fiscal policy process is relatively cooperative between the president and the Congress if a unified government occurs in which one party controls both branches. The executive and legislative branches are likely to agree on the direction and composition of fiscal policy in a unified government of one-party control.

Suppose the Republican party controls the executive and legislative branches. This happens if the president and a majority of legislators in the House and the Senate are members of the Republican party. A unified conservative government occurs. Consequently, the fiscal policy is likely to be conservative. A conservative fiscal policy emphasizes a relatively small size of government. This occurs through relatively low government spending (especially reduced social programs rather than reduced military spending) for a contractionary fiscal policy and relatively low taxes for an expansionary fiscal policy.

Fiscal policy is likely to be liberal if the Democratic party controls the legislature and the presidency. A unified liberal government occurs in this instance. A liberal fiscal policy supports a relatively larger role of government in the economy. A liberal expansionary fiscal policy consists of relatively high government expenditure, especially on social programs. A liberal contractionary fiscal policy consists of relatively high progressivity of income taxes on businesses and households.

Suppose the president is a member of one party, while most members of the House and the Senate are members of the opposing political party. A power split occurs on political party control of the two government branches. A divided government arises. For example, the president may be a Democrat while most members of the Congress are Republicans. The president is unlikely to fully attain the desired fiscal policy in a divided government. The fiscal policy is likely to be conflictual in a condition of political gridlock. The majority of members of the Congress and the president are likely to clash on the level and distribution of government spending and taxes.

Monetary Policy: Money Supply and Interest Rates

The Federal Reserve is the central bank and monetary authority in the U.S. economy. The duty of Fed is to administer monetary policy and regulate the banking system. Monetary policy is the control of money supply and interest rates to promote a strong economy with stable low inflation. Monetary policy impacts aggregate demand, with short- and long-run effects on unemployment, inflation, RGDP, and the dynamics of the business cycle. The policy is primarily administered through open market operations (OMO). It is also sometimes administered through Fed purchases of long-term private assets, such as mortgage-backed securities. This is called quantitative easing[1].

The Federal Open Market Committee (FOMC) is the decision-making body of the Fed that is in charge of monetary policy. The FOMC consists of 12 members. The FOMC chairperson is the chairperson of the Board of Governors of the Federal Reserve System. The president appoints the Fed chairperson (of the Board of Governors of the Federal Reserve System) to

---

[1] The discount rate and the reserve requirement also affect money supply and interest rates. These two instruments, however, are not the main tools of monetary policy.

serve renewable four-year terms. The other FOMC members consist of six members of the Board of Governors, plus the president of the Federal Reserve Bank of New York, and four additional Federal Reserve district bank presidents who serve rotating one-year terms.

This somewhat complex and rotating configuration of FOMC members establishes diversity and plurality in the money supply decision-making process. This mechanism operates as a partial safeguard against excessive control over monetary policy by special interests, the president, the Congress, and the political parties.

Money Supply and Interest Rates

Money supply consists of cash held outside of banks plus bank account deposits. Most of the money supply is in the form of bank deposits, such as checking accounts, savings accounts, and bank certificates of deposit. The Fed uses several different measurements for the quantity of money in the economy, such as M1, M2, M3, and L. The M2 definition of money supply is a widely used measure. M2 consists of cash held outside of banks plus checking and savings account deposits. Money supply is measured nominally and in real terms.

The nominal money supply is the total dollar value of the amount of money in circulation. Real money supply is a measure of purchasing power. Real money supply is the value of money in relation to the prices of products throughout the economy. Real money supply equals nominal money supply divided by the aggregate price index. The aggregate price index is an indicator of the average price level of new products (see Chapter 2 for a discussion on nominal and real values). Real money supply is also called real balances.

A cause–effect relation occurs between real money supply and interest rates. Higher real money supply causes lower interest rates. Lower real money supply leads to higher interest rates. The price of money, especially from a borrower's perspective, may be thought of as the interest rate. The interest rate and interest payments on loans reflect the price or cost of borrowing money.

According to economic market analysis, an increase in the supply of a product causes its price to decline. Alternatively, when the supply of an economic good decreases, its price goes up. Based on this concept, an inverse relation occurs between the real money supply and its price, which is the interest rate. A change in real money supply affects the interest rate. An increase in the supply of real money causes its price, the interest rate, to go down. A decrease in the real money supply causes the interest rate to go up.

Figure 4.3 shows the general inverse pattern between real balances and interest rates in the U.S. economy. The scatter graph in Figure 4.3 measures the interest rate for AAA corporate bonds along the vertical axis and the growth rate for the real M2 money supply along the horizontal axis. The economic data consists of monthly observations across the time frame from August 1992 to January 2015. The scatterplot shows a general inverse relation. This is indicated by the downward trend line. As the growth rate of real money supply goes up, the interest rate goes down. This inverse pattern signifies money demand. The money demand pattern, however, is not perfectly correlated with all the observations in the graph. Many of the data points in the scatter graph occur above and below the trend line. This occurs because other economic determinants (besides the interest rate) also affect the demand for money.

Besides the interest rate, RGDP is an important factor on money demand. RGDP has a positive impact on money demand and interest rates.

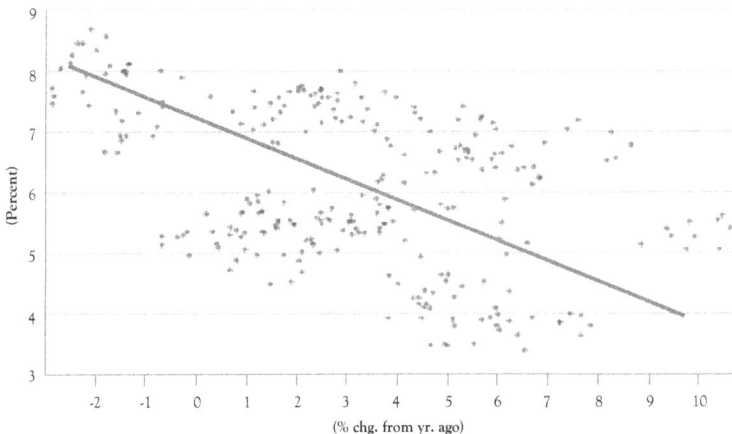

Figure 4.3 Real M2 money supply and the interest rate

Source: Federal Reserve Economic Data (FRED)

Higher RGDP creates a higher demand for money. A greater amount of money is needed in a growing economy to accommodate more spending. This effect is called the transactions demand for money.

Higher money demand connected with higher income and RGDP tends to cause higher interest rates. According to economic market analysis, an increase in the demand for a good will cause its price to rise. The price of money is the interest rate. A higher demand for money causes its price to rise, which is the interest rate. Alternatively, lower RGDP causes money demand to fall. In this case, less money is demanded because of less income and less spending. Interest rates therefore tend to go down.

Open Market Operations

Monetary policy mainly occurs through open market operations (OMO) as determined by the Federal Open Market Committee (FOMC) of the Fed. The OMO mechanism involves central bank purchases and sales of government securities, such as treasury bonds or T-bonds. This action affects money supply and interest rates. Expansionary open market operations consist of Fed purchases of T-bonds. The Fed pays for T-bonds by printing new currency. When the Fed buys T-bonds from the public in the secondary bond market, an injection of cash occurs in the economy and in the banking system as bank reserves. Cash held by banks is called reserves. Through expansionary OMO, banks obtain more cash reserves to lend to business and household borrowers. Bank loans thus increase. When bank loans increase, the money supply in the economy also increases.

Banks earn interest income by lending to households and businesses. To increase the amount of loans, however, banks typically reduce interest rates to induce households and firms to borrow more funds for consumer spending, residential investment, and business investment. More bank loans lead to an expansion in business and residential investments as well as an increase in debt-financed consumer spending. Consequently, an expansionary or loose OMO policy creates higher macroeconomic demand in the form of higher consumer expenditure and more economic investment spending. RGDP accordingly rises and unemployment declines as macroeconomic demand goes up. This outcome of higher RGDP and lower unemployment is the main goal of loose monetary policy. A negative side effect of expansionary monetary policy is higher inflation. Inflation likely increases because of higher macroeconomic demand. Buyers are willing to pay higher product prices when demand increases.

In addition to an expansionary OMO, the central bank may sometimes adopt quantitative easing. This consists of Fed purchases of long-term private bonds to increase the money supply. For example, the central bank may print new cash to buy mortgage-backed securities. This has a similar effect on money supply and interest rates as an expansionary OMO. Central bank purchases of mortgage-backed securities create an injection of cash into the economy. Much of this new cash ends up as reserves in banks. These new bank reserves allow more bank loans to occur. Money supply therefore expands, and interest rates decline.

A contractionary or tight OMO has an opposite effect. A contractionary OMO policy consists of the Fed selling T-bonds to the public in the secondary bond market. The Fed receives money as it sells T-bonds to bond dealers. This action causes money to exit the economy into the vaults of the Fed. A leakage of money occurs from the economy and the banking system. Less cash or reserves are available in banks to lend to borrowers. Bank loans decline and money supply decreases.

This fall in money supply tends to drive up interest rates. A lower supply of money causes its price to rise, which is the interest rate. Higher interest rates create a contractionary demand effect on consumer spending and business investment. Higher interest rates make consumer and business borrowing more expensive. Debt-financed investment and consumption decrease. As aggregate demand falls, inflation goes down. Lower inflation is the goal of tight monetary policy. A negative side effect of a tight monetary policy is lower RGDP and higher unemployment. RGDP and unemployment likely worsen because of lower aggregate demand.

The characteristics of expansionary and contractionary monetary policies are summarized in Table 4.2.

An important characteristic of the money supply process is the fractional reserve banking system. Money supply increases through the process of bank loans. When an individual or business borrows from a bank, the money supply goes up by the amount of the loan or the debt. This implies that a large portion of the money supply is related to the amount

Table 4.2 Expansionary and contractionary monetary policies

Type of monetary policy	Loose policy	Tight policy
OMO	Net purchase of T-bonds	Net sale of T-bonds
Effect upon bank reserves	Increase in bank reserves	Decrease in bank reserves
Effect upon bank loans	Increase in bank loans	Decrease in bank loans
Effect upon real money supply	Increase in real money supply growth	Decrease in real money supply growth
Effect upon interest rates	Decrease in interest rates	Increase in interest rates
Macroeconomic goals	Higher RGDP, lower unemployment	Lower inflation
Macroeconomic side effect	Higher inflation	Macroeconomic slowdown, possible recession
Macroeconomic problem that the policy addresses	Recession or slow macro-economic growth	High inflation

of private debt in the economy. Money creation through bank loans can create an economic vulnerability. Periodically, substantial bank loan defaults occur in the economy, such as the mortgage financial crisis of the Great Recession in 2007–2009. When a large amount of bank loan defaults occurs, the money supply declines proportionately. This adversely affects macroeconomic demand, GDP, and unemployment.

Monetary Policy Targeting of Inflation and Interest Rates

The central bank sets targets for inflation and interest rates (and other macroeconomic indicators) in determining monetary policy. The Fed tends to emphasize one or the other macroeconomic targets at different times. The monetary policy goal of inflation targeting focuses on the attainment of low, stable inflation. Inflation targeting is particularly applicable when the economy suffers from high inflation. In addition, the political right and classicalism often emphasize inflation targeting because of its implications for a stable business and financial environment. A stable, low inflation rate reduces financial risk, which enables market forces to flourish. Market forces operate more efficiently in a steady financial setting. This promotes stronger long-run economic growth.

The other main monetary policy objective is interest rate targeting. This strategy focuses on maintaining low and stable interest rates. Low interest rates reduce the cost of borrowing. This permits greater business and residential investment and higher consumer spending. Aggregate demand consequently rises. This leads to stronger RGDP growth and declining unemployment. The political left and Keynesianism tend to emphasize interest rate targeting, especially during episodes of macroeconomic slowdown.

Fiscal and Monetary Policy Coordination and Time Lags

Two additional issues are macroeconomic policy coordination and time lags in macroeconomic policy. The first issue is policy coordination. Depending on the macroeconomic preferences of the policymakers, the fiscal and monetary policies may reinforce each other. Alternatively, the two macroeconomic policies may conflict and could even offset each other.

The fiscal and monetary policies reinforce each other if the three macroeconomic policymakers agree on the policy direction. This occurs if the Fed, the president, and the Congress are unified on whether macroeconomic policies should be expansionary or contractionary. For example, a coordinated set of expansionary macroeconomic policies consists of tax cuts or higher government spending as determined by the president and the Congress combined with higher money supply growth and lower interest rates as adopted by the central bank.

Alternatively, the macroeconomic policymakers may disagree on the direction of stabilization policy. For example, Congress and the president may adopt an expansionary fiscal policy, while the Fed adopts a contractionary monetary policy. The two policies, in this instance, oppose each other. The net effect on the economy could consequently cancel out.

The other issue, besides policy coordination, is time lags for fiscal and monetary policies. Fiscal policy has a quicker impact than monetary policy. Tax cuts and higher government spending have a faster effect on the economy than higher money supply growth and lower interest rates.

Higher government spending or lower taxes impact RGDP and unemployment over a period of several months. Higher government spending directly causes higher GDP since government spending is a GDP component. Lower taxes also influence the economy relatively fast. The tax effect, however, is indirect. Lower income taxes directly influence disposable income. Higher disposable income then affects consumer spending, which is a component of GDP.

The effect of monetary policy on the economy, on the other hand, may require one year or longer to fully occur. Several linkages must take place over time for monetary policy. First, open market operations impact the amount of reserves held in banks. Higher bank reserves allow more bank loans to occur. The money supply rises as bank loans to businesses and households increase. Correspondingly, interest rates decline as money supply increases. Lower interest rates enable more consumer and business borrowing. Debt-financed consumer spending and business investment spending consequently expand. Finally, GDP increases and the unemployment rate falls.

CHAPTER 5

Voter Rationality and Macroeconomic Preferences

Introduction: Rational Voting, Rational Ignorance, and Political Parties

Rational voter theory asserts that citizens generally cast votes based on a rational decision-making process (Downs 1957). The political opinion-making process involves a subjective cost–benefit analysis by voters. Citizens rationally consider the different policy platforms among the political candidates and political parties. Citizens vote for the politician who supports the set of policies that offer the greatest perceived political net benefit. Individuals vote for the political candidate whose policies most closely resemble their own political preferences. A citizen's political preference is the most preferred political outcome.

However, becoming fully informed on political and economic issues, and developing well-thought-out opinions is time-consuming and costly. Individuals often do not devote enough time and other resources to become completely informed on all relevant politico-economic matters that affect them. Rational ignorance consequently occurs. Rational ignorance refers to a voter's decision to remain partially uninformed on some political issues because the costs of becoming more politically aware exceed the added benefits from gaining a more-informed opinion.

Political parties play an important role in rational ignorance. Some citizens simply vote for their preferred political party. A voter's preferred political party is the party that most closely aligns with the voter's overall political viewpoint. Voting for the politician who is a member of the preferred political party is straightforward. This process is less costly than the alternative approach of developing a fully informed opinion about all the political candidates. Voting for the candidate of the preferred political party is less complex than becoming knowledgeable of all policy proposals from all candidates.

Normal Distribution of Voter Preferences: The Partisan Model and the Median Voter Model

Voters form political views and cast votes based on a subjective cost–benefit analysis of the issues, political candidates, and political parties. The median voter is the middle voter within the overall range of citizen political preferences. Figure 5.1 shows the distribution of voter preferences with respect to the median voter and the left and right political parties.

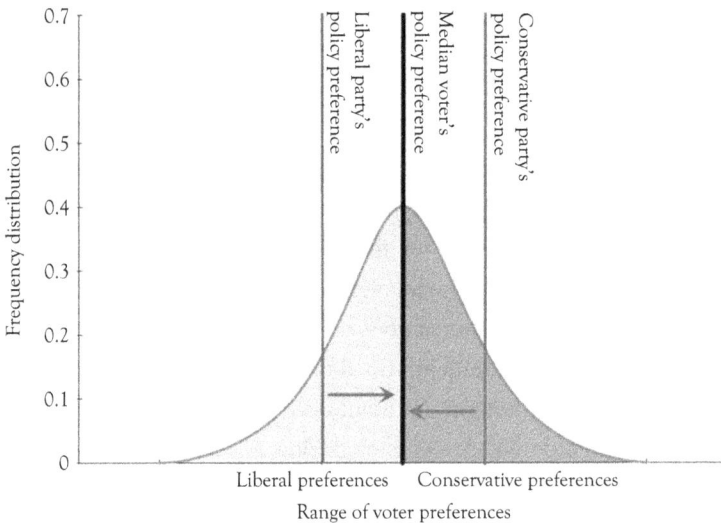

Figure 5.1 Political party platforms and the median voter model

The bell-shaped curve in Figure 5.1 is the distribution of voter preferences for a public policy, such as macroeconomic policy. The diagram shows a normal distribution of voter preferences as demonstrated by the bell-shaped curve. The frequency distribution of voter preferences is measured along the vertical axis, and the range of voter policy preferences is measured along the horizontal axis.

Voters with political preferences toward the right side of the horizontal axis are relatively conservative in political orientation. Voter preferences toward the left side of the horizontal scale are relatively liberal. Voter preferences are increasingly conservative moving from left to right along the horizontal axis. Voter preferences become more liberal moving from right to left. The vertical line at the center peak of the preference distribution is the median voter's most preferred political outcome.

Partisan Influence Model and the Macroeconomy

Two vertical lines appear to the right and left of the median voter's preference. The two lines signify the policy positions of the conservative and liberal political parties. The partisan influence theory asserts that the left and right political parties support policies to the left and right of the center of the voter preference distribution. These two partisan positions align with the preferences of the core constituencies of the left and right parties.

The political parties seek to maximize financial support and approval from their core constituencies. Elected officials place greater emphasis on partisan-related interests rather than the overall sentiment of all voters. The two main parties embrace polices that appeal to their core constituencies instead of the median voter's preference. The policy stances of the two parties consequently remain stable at the left and right vertical lines. A partisan divide occurs in the policies of the two parties.

For example, a conservative macroeconomic preference places a strong emphasis on maintaining low inflation relative to unemployment. A liberal macroeconomic preference focuses on low unemployment compared to inflation. Partisan macroeconomic theory suggests that the president embraces policies that align with the partisan macroeconomic agenda. Democratic presidents support policies that emphasize low unemployment. Republican incumbents support policies that focus on low inflation.

Median Voter Model and the Macroeconomy

In addition to the partisan influence model, the other main framework for political party behavior is the median voter model. The median voter model considers the role of political parties and the objective of politicians to win elections. The median voter theory suggests that politicians modify their opinions and actions over time to align with the median voter's most preferred political outcome. This happens regardless of the politician or the political party in power.

Let us once again refer to a normal distribution of citizen preferences. The initial political party preferences occur at the right and left vertical lines in Figure 5.1. Now, assume that the conservative political party seeks to increase its vote share in an upcoming election. The conservative party vote share is the fraction of the two-party vote in favor of the conservative political candidate. The liberal party vote share is the fraction of the two-party vote in favor of the liberal candidate. The two-party vote is the sum of votes for the conservative candidate plus the liberal candidate.

To increase the vote share for the conservative candidate, the conservative party shifts its policy stance to the left toward the median voter's preference. The conservative political party consequently induces some centrist voters to switch their vote from the liberal candidate to the conservative politician. The liberal political party observes this strategy and responds by shifting its policy position more to the right toward the median voter so as not to lose votes. A political competition occurs between the two parties as each side seeks to increase its vote share. Each political party moves its policy position closer toward the center until both political parties end up with similar policies coinciding with the median voter's preference.

In the long run, the political party that is elected becomes largely irrelevant in a competitive political market. To maximize votes and approval ratings, the two major political parties and the associated political candidates end up adopting similar policies that match the median voter's most preferred outcome.

Consider the median voter model in terms of macroeconomic policy. The median voter's macroeconomic preference is the median person's opinion of ideal macroeconomic performance. This preference consists of an unemployment target and an inflation target. The targets reflect the median citizen's opinion of ideal unemployment and ideal inflation.

Suppose the median voter's preference consists of an inflation target of 3 percent and an unemployment target of 5 percent. The median voter's economic well-being is maximized if actual economic performance ends up being equal to this preferred outcome. Alternatively, the median individual's satisfaction declines if the economy ends up deviating from this median preference. In the median voter model, the president (regardless of political party) supports macroeconomic policies that attain the median voter's inflation and unemployment targets. This policy strategy seeks to maximize approval ratings and increase reelection prospects.

Time-Consistent Macroeconomic Preference

The median voter model asserts that the president supports policies that attain the median voter's macroeconomic preference. This enables the president to increase approval ratings and reelection votes. The median preference may be time consistent or time inconsistent. A time-consistent (or dynamically consistent) macroeconomic preference is farsighted. The preference is compatible with the long-run potential of the economy. A consistent macroeconomic preference is sustainable. The sustainable unemployment target is equal to the natural unemployment rate. The natural rate is the lowest level of unemployment the economy can maintain over an extended period of time.

Let us assume the median voter's preference consists of an unemployment target equal to the natural rate (of say 5 percent) and an inflation target of 3 percent. This is point A in Figure 5.2. This occurs at

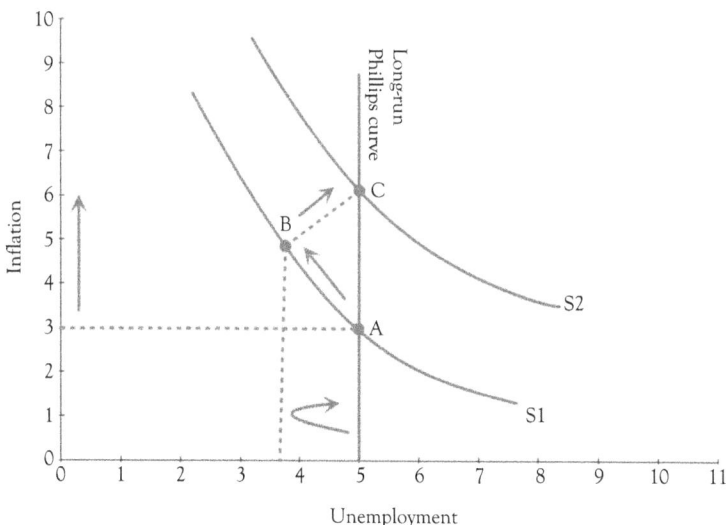

Figure 5.2 Macroeconomic time consistency versus inconsistency

the intersection between the long-run Phillips curve and the short-run Phillips curve, S1. The median voter's macroeconomic preference is dynamically consistent and sustainable. The preference is consistent because it occurs at a point on the long-run Phillips curve. The economy can maintain this level of performance in the absence of economic shocks. The incumbent maximizes popularity and reelection votes by supporting macroeconomic policies that attain point A.

Time-Inconsistent Macroeconomic Preference

Now, consider what happens if the median voter's macroeconomic preference is dynamically inconsistent. The median voter's preference is incompatible with the long-run capabilities of the economy. Dynamic inconsistency arises if the median voter's unemployment target is less than the natural unemployment rate. An unemployment target less than the natural rate is shortsighted or unsustainable. Dynamic inconsistency occurs if the median voter does not recognize the long-run potential of the economy. The median voter may be uninformed about the level of macroeconomic performance that is possible over the long term.

Let us assume the median voter's preference is inconsistent and that the president embraces policy to attain the median voter's inconsistent macroeconomic preference. Stabilization policy that seeks to maintain an unemployment target that is less than the natural rate is not feasible. An inconsistent unemployment target triggers economic overheating and rising inflation. To show this result, suppose the economy is initially at point A in Figure 5.2. Let us also assume the median voter's preference is equal to an unemployment target of 3.75 percent and an inflation target of 5 percent. This inconsistent preference is shown as point B in Figure 5.2.

Expansionary stabilization policy can temporarily attain this level of economic performance. Through expansionary policy, the economy moves up and to the left along the short-run Phillips curve S1 from point A to point B where the inconsistent preference is realized. Point B, however, is not sustainable. Point B is a temporary outcome that cannot be maintained. Pressures in the labor market build up. This causes inflationary expectations and the wage rate to rise. Workers seek higher wages to compensate for higher product prices associated with the movement from point A to point B. As wage costs go up, the Phillips curve shifts right from S1 to S2. The higher labor costs cause businesses to reduce output and jobs. This causes unemployment to rise and return to the sustainable natural rate of 5 percent. Additionally, firms shift the burden of higher labor costs to consumers in the form of higher product prices. Inflation rises to about 6 percent. The economy adjusts to point C in the long term.

Table 5.1 summarizes macroeconomic consistency versus macroeconomic inconsistency.

Table 5.1 Dynamic macroeconomic consistency and inconsistency

Median voter's macroeconomic preference	Median voter's unemployment target	Macroeconomic results
Time-inconsistent macroeconomic preference	Unemployment target is less than the natural unemployment rate	Unsustainable unemployment target; economic overheating and rising inflation occur; the unemployment rate returns to the natural rate in the long run
Time-consistent macroeconomic preference	Unemployment target is equal to the natural unemployment rate	Unemployment target is sustainable in the long run

Macroeconomic Inconsistency and the Electoral Cycle

The electoral political business cycle effect may occur if macroeconomic inconsistency takes place. The electoral cycle effect assumes the median voter's macroeconomic preference is dynamically inconsistent. The median voter's unemployment target, in this case, is less than the natural rate. Consequently, the president may decide to embrace opportunistic policy to temporarily attain the median voter's inconsistent preference. The president and the incumbent political party can increase reelection votes by adopting opportunistic policy that temporarily reduces unemployment below the natural rate in an election year. The president engineers an economic expansion prior to the election to increase reelection votes. This short-term favorable economic outcome, however, comes at the cost of greater inflation after the presidential election.

The opposite result occurs if the median voter's macroeconomic preference is time consistent and farsighted. A decline in unemployment below the natural rate prior to an election causes a decrease (rather than increase) in the presidential reelection vote share. In this case, overly expansive macroeconomic policy is recognized as an attempt to create a temporary economic boom that comes at the cost of higher inflation after the election. If the median voter's macroeconomic preference is far-sighted, then macroeconomic opportunism by the president fails to increase reelection votes.

Bimodal Distribution of Preferences, Protest Vote Abstention, and the Partisan Influence Model

Let us consider the policy outcome that could develop in a bimodal distribution of voter preferences. In this case, the partisan effect may occur rather than the median voter effect. In this instance, two peaks or modes occur within the bimodal range of voter preferences. The two modes align with the policy preferences of the liberal and conservative core constituencies. Voter sentiment is split into two major camps that take place at the two modes to the left and right of the median voter's preference.

The partisan effect based on a bimodal distribution of voter macroeconomic preferences is shown in Figure 5.3.

In a bimodal distribution of voter preferences, the policy platforms of the left and right parties may not converge to the center as predicted by the median voter model. Instead, the political party platforms may remain stable at the two modes in the preference distribution.

In figure 5.3, the conservative party preference is the right vertical line and the liberal party policy preference is the left vertical line. The policy preferences of the two parties do not converge to the median voter's preference if protest vote abstention arises. Protest vote abstention occurs if far-wing voters abstain from voting as a protest against the political parties.

Protest vote abstention happens if a political party shifts its policies too close to the center. Some right-wing voters abstain from voting if the right party moves its policy too close to the middle. Some left-wing voters refrain from voting out of protest if the left party shifts its policy platform too close to the center. Consequently, to prevent a loss of votes from far-wing supporters, the two political parties maintain their policy platforms at the two peaks to the left and right of the median voter's preference.

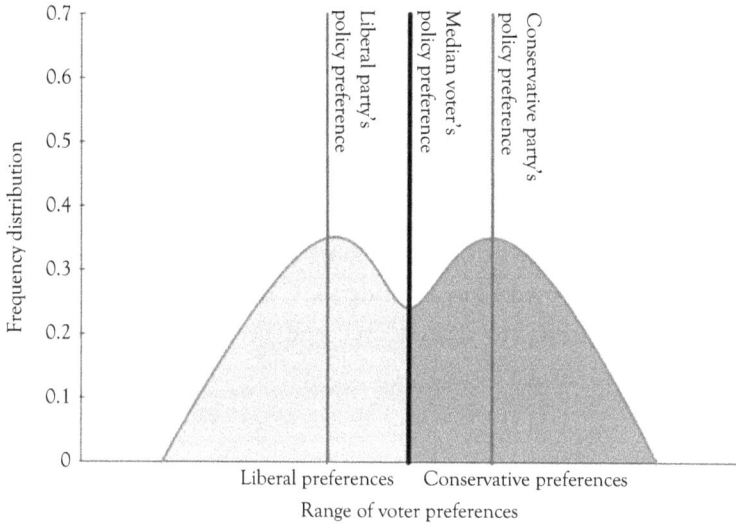

Figure 5.3 Bimodal distribution of voter preferences

Rational Vote Abstention

A related concept is rational vote abstention. A percentage of citizens refrain from voting if they consider their vote as inconsequential in an election outcome. Some citizens choose not to vote because the costs of voting outweigh the perceived influence of their vote on an election result. Rational vote abstention may or may not impact an election outcome. If rational vote abstention occurs evenly across the range of voters on both the political right and the political left, then the election outcome is unchanged.

If rational vote abstention is concentrated across a narrow range of voters, however, then the effect could impact an election result. For example, suppose rational vote abstention occurs primarily among liberal voters. The election outcome is consequently swayed in favor of the conservative candidate. If rational vote abstention mainly occurs among conservative voters, then the election vote outcome shifts more in favor of the liberal candidate.

Conclusion

This chapter discusses voter rationality and political parties in the median voter framework. We also consider dynamic consistency versus dynamic inconsistency in the expectational Phillips curve model. We discuss the median voter model and dynamic inconsistency in relation to the electoral cycle effect. Additionally, we examine the partisan macroeconomic model in the context of a normal distribution and a bimodal distribution of voter preferences. Finally, we discuss the influence of protest vote abstention and rational vote abstention on election outcomes. Chapter 6 examines the electoral cycle effect in more detail. Chapter 7 looks at the partisan influence model in greater detail. Chapter 8 examines the U.S. economy for evidence of partisan cycle and electoral cycle effects from 1961 to 2016.

CHAPTER 6

Electoral Political Business Cycle

Introduction: Political Business Cycle Effects

The political business cycle (PBC) literature examines electoral, partisan, and other political influences on the macroeconomic policy and the economy. PBC analysis focuses on the issue of presidential manipulation of the macroeconomic policy for political reasons, such as incumbent reelection ambition and partisan economic goals.

The median voter model on the macroeconomy is discussed in Chapter 5. This model asserts that the president supports stabilization policies that move the economy toward the median voter's macroeconomic preference as a strategy to increase presidential job approval and in-party presidential reelection votes. Two related PBC effects may also occur. They are the electoral cycle and the partisan cycle. This chapter discusses the electoral cycle, while Chapter 7 considers the partisan cycle. Chapter 8 then examines the U.S. economy for evidence of electoral and partisan PBC effects during Democratic and Republican presidencies.

Macroeconomic Time Inconsistency and the Electoral Cycle

A large body of research shows that the economy affects presidential job approval as well as presidential and congressional election outcomes (see Chapter 9). The median voter model suggests election votes are highest for the political candidate whose policy platform most closely aligns with the median voter's macroeconomic preference.

The outcome of macroeconomic policy depends on whether the median voter's preference is dynamically consistent or inconsistent (see Kydland and Prescott 1977, for a discussion of macroeconomic time inconsistency). The median macroeconomic preference is either consistent or inconsistent based on the median unemployment target, which reflects the median voter's opinion of the optimal or ideal unemployment rate.

If the median preference is time consistent, then the median voter is well-informed on the economy and farsighted. The median citizen recognizes the basic structure of the economy and supports a policy consistent with the long-run potential of the economy. The median voter's expectations of the macroeconomy are realistic. The preference is dynamically consistent if the median voter's unemployment target equals the efficient level of unemployment. The efficient level of unemployment is the natural rate. The president supports a policy that attains optimal long-run macroeconomic performance if the median voter's preference is dynamically consistent. The president supports a policy that attains the natural unemployment rate.

If the median macroeconomic preference is dynamically inconsistent, then the median voter is uninformed on the macroeconomic structure. The median voter's macroeconomic expectations are unrealistic and naïve. The median voter overestimates macroeconomic potential. An inconsistent macroeconomic preference occurs if the median voter's unemployment target is less than the natural unemployment rate. A government policy that seeks to attain an inconsistent macroeconomic preference yields only a temporary decline in unemployment below the natural rate but with higher inflation in the long term.

The electoral cycle effect may occur if the median voter's unemployment target is less than the natural rate. The median voter's preference, in this case, is dynamically inconsistent. The electoral cycle occurs from presidential manipulation of the stabilization policy to create a transitory economic boom in an election year to increase reelection votes. The median voter's macroeconomic preference must be dynamically inconsistent for an electoral-cycle policy to succeed in its aim to increase presidential reelection votes. In the electoral cycle, the median citizen is shortsighted and naively approves of a policy that attains a temporary decline in unemployment prior to the presidential election that cannot be sustained afterward. The median voter is unaware on the adverse effect of higher long-term inflation that develops from an opportunistic macroeconomic policy.

However, if the median voter's preference is dynamically consistent, then macroeconomic overstimulation in an election year causes the presidential reelection vote share for the in-party to decline rather than increase. Farsighted voters oppose an opportunistic policy because of the economic distortions that occur. Farsighted citizens vote against the in-party if the incumbent pursues an electoral-cycle macroeconomic policy.

The question of whether the median voter is macroeconomically shortsighted or farsighted is an empirical matter. This hypothesis is tested by estimating the presidential vote equation as well as other empirical equations of citizen sentiment. The issue of estimating whether the median voter's macroeconomic preference is dynamically consistent or inconsistent will be addressed in Chapter 10. The characteristics of macroeconomic time consistency versus macroeconomic time inconsistency in relation to the electoral cycle are summarized in Table 6.1.

Table 6.1 Opportunistic policy and macroeconomic inconsistency

Median voter's macroeconomic preference	Median voter's unemployment target	Macroeconomic outcomes	Impact of an opportunistic policy on presidential reelection votes
Time-inconsistent macroeconomic preference	Unemployment target is less than the natural unemployment rate	Unemployment target is unsustainable; economic overheating and inflation will occur	An opportunistic policy causes an increase in the vote share for the incumbent party
Time-consistent macroeconomic preference	Unemployment target equals the natural unemployment rate	Unemployment target is sustainable; economic overheating will not occur	An opportunistic policy causes a decrease in the vote share for the incumbent party

Electoral Cycle: Asymmetric Information and the Principal–Agent Problem

Some research on the electoral cycle effect include Nordhaus, (1975), Lindbeck (1976), McRae (1977), and Tufte (1978). The electoral cycle assumes macroeconomic ignorance or short-sightedness by voters, in other words macroeconomic inconsistency. This voter characteristic is combined with an opportunistic stabilization policy orchestrated by the president to increase reelection votes for the in-party. The electoral cycle therefore assumes asymmetrical macroeconomic information between the in-party and voters.

The president and the in-party are more economically informed than the general populace. The incumbent (mis)uses this informational advantage to manipulate short-term macroeconomic outcomes to boost approval ratings and gain more reelection votes. The lopsided information disparity between the incumbent political party and voters forms a principal–agent problem. The incumbent is the principal, while voters are the agents. The economic manipulation of less-informed agents (voters) by the more-informed principal (incumbent and in-party) forms the basis for the electoral cycle.

The electoral cycle pattern occurs in two stages. Each of the two phases involves short-run and long-run economic effects. The first phase involves a preelection opportunistic macroeconomic policy. The second phase involves a postelection anti-inflation policy. Figure 6.1 shows the

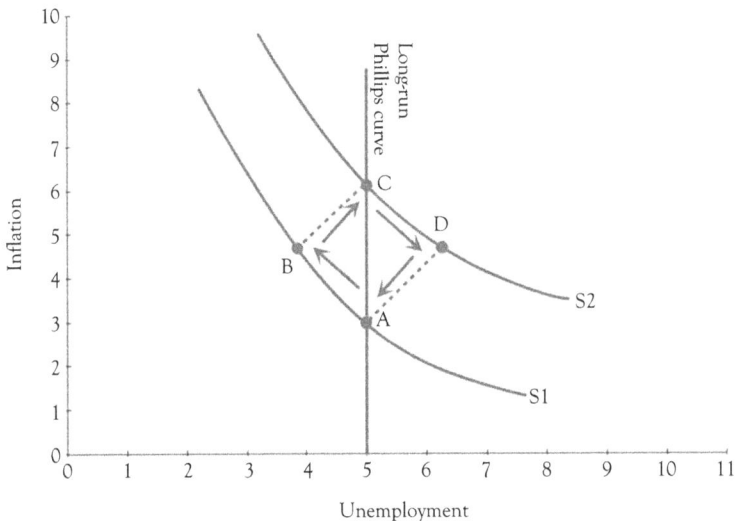

Figure 6.1 Electoral cycle

dynamics of the two phases of the electoral cycle in the expectational Phillips curve framework.

Let us assume the economy is initially in long-run equilibrium at point A. This occurs at the intersection between the short-run Phillips curve, S1, and the vertical long-run Phillips curve. Unemployment is initially at the natural rate, while inflation is about 3 percent.

Short-Run and Long-Run Effects in Preelection Phase

In the first stage of the electoral cycle, the incumbent engineers an expansionary policy in the election year. The expansionary policy consists of fiscal measures or monetary measures or both. Presidential manipulation of the macroeconomic policy, however, is partial and indirect. As discussed in Chapter 4, the president in association with the Congress and the political parties determine the fiscal policy, while the central bank directly determines the monetary policy. The Congress and the Fed must accommodate the opportunistic policy agenda of the incumbent for the electoral-cycle effect to take place.

An expansionary fiscal policy consists of higher government spending or lower taxes. Higher government expenditure directly adds jobs and output to the economy. Lower taxes indirectly lead to greater GDP and more jobs. Lower taxes create more household and business after-tax income. This enables more consumer and business expenditures. An expansionary monetary policy consists of higher real money supply growth and lower real interest rates. A loose monetary policy spurs business and residential investment and consumer spending because of cheaper borrowing costs.

Opportunistic expansionary macroeconomic policies cause higher aggregate demand and a preelection economic boom toward the end of a four-year presidential term. Real economic growth rises and unemployment declines. The economy moves upward to the left along the short-run Phillips curve, S1, from point A to point B in the election year. Unemployment falls to around 4 percent as shown in Figure 6.1. This economic expansion improves the financial well-being of citizens. Consequently, voters approve of the president and the reelection vote share increases for the incumbent. Or the vote share increases for the new in-party presidential candidate if the incumbent is retiring after two terms in office.

If the economy grows sufficiently through expansive macroeconomic policies at the end of a presidential term, then the in-party wins reelection to the White House as intended by the opportunistic policy. Rising inflation, however, occurs alongside declining unemployment. This is shown by the movement from point A to point B in Figure 6.1. Inflation rises from 3 percent to about 5 percent. Higher macroeconomic demand from an expansionary policy leads to greater consumer and business spending on goods and services. This drives up product prices.

In the long run of the first stage of the electoral cycle, the Phillips curve shifts rightward from S1 to S2. The economy moves from point B to point C. This occurs through the self-correcting mechanism of market forces. Much of this adjustment takes place after the election. The labor market responds to economic overheating caused by preelection expansionary measures. Workers increase their inflation expectations and demand higher wages to pay for higher product prices caused by higher macroeconomic demand. Business firms react to higher labor costs by cutting employment and production. Unemployment rises and adjusts back toward the natural unemployment rate of 5 percent in the long run. Additionally, inflation rises further to about 6 percent. This occurs as higher labor costs are pushed to consumers in the form of higher product prices. The long-run adverse effects of the electoral cycle are higher inflation with no permanent decline in the unemployment rate below the natural rate.

Short-Run and Long-Run Effects in the Second Phase

A contractionary policy is adopted after the presidential election to alleviate macroeconomic overheating caused by preelection economic overstimulus. A contractionary fiscal policy consists of higher taxes or lower government spending. A tight monetary policy consists of lower money supply growth and higher real interest rates. A tight monetary policy leads to higher interest rates and lower debt-financed consumption and investment spending. Contractionary stabilization policies create lower macroeconomic demand. This is shown as a movement down and to the right along the short-run Phillips curve, S2, from point C to point D in Figure 6.1. Inflation declines from 6 percent to about 4½ percent.

Lower macroeconomic demand causes producers to reduce prices to induce buyers to purchase products.

A postelection economic slowdown takes place. Unemployment rises from 5 percent to around 6½ percent. This is shown by the movement from point C to point D. Anti-inflationary stabilization policies come at the cost of a postelection economic slump. Unemployment worsens because of lower macroeconomic demand associated with a contractionary policy.

The Phillips curve shifts left from S2 to S1 in the long run of the second phase of the electoral cycle. The economy moves from point D to point A. Inflation continues to fall from around 4½ percent to about 3 percent as the economic slowdown is eventually alleviated through the self-correcting mechanism. The labor market reacts to lower macroeconomic demand caused by a contractionary policy. Workers reduce inflationary expectations and reduce demand for higher wages because of the slowing rate of product inflation. The decrease in real wages enables business firms to increase output and jobs. This leads to lower unemployment. Unemployment eventually returns to the natural rate of 5 percent in the long run.

Summary of the Electoral Cycle

In the initial stage of the electoral cycle, opportunistic policies cause higher economic growth, lower unemployment, and perhaps some increase in inflation prior to an election. Lower unemployment and higher economic growth cause an increase in the in-party presidential reelection vote share. The economic gain of lower unemployment is temporary. In the long run of the initial phase of the electoral cycle, inflation rises even further as higher wage costs are transferred to buyers in the form of higher prices. After the election, unemployment increases toward the natural rate through the self-correcting mechanism of market forces.

In the second phase of the electoral cycle, a contractionary policy is adopted after the election. This reduces inflation caused by the preelection economic expansion. A contractionary policy also causes an economic slowdown. In the long run of the second phase, the self-correcting mechanism causes real wages and expected inflation to adjust downward to match the decline in actual product price inflation. The adjustment of wages to prices alleviates the economic slowdown and unemployment returns to the natural rate in the long run.

Table 6.2 summarizes the short-run and long-run economic and political effects of the two phases of the electoral cycle.

Table 6.2 Electoral cycle effects

Electoral cycle stages	Time frame	Macroeconomic policy	Objective	Short-run effects	Long-run effects
First phase	Prior to the presidential election	Expansionary macroeconomic policy	Improve economic performance and win presidential reelection	Rising economic growth, falling unemployment, rising inflation	Further increase in inflation; no permanent decline in unemployment
Second phase	Following the presidential election	Contractionary macroeconomic policy	Alleviate inflation caused by preelection economic overheating	Disinflation, rising unemployment, declining economic growth	Further decline in inflation; unemployment falls and returns to the natural rate

A corresponding set of effects occur for the fiscal and monetary policies in connection with the electoral cycle of the economy. In the electoral cycle, expansionary fiscal and monetary policies occur prior to the presidential election to expand the economy and increase in-party reelection votes. Following the election, contractionary fiscal and monetary policies are adopted to bring down inflation caused by the preelection economic stimulus.

An opportunistic fiscal policy creates the political budget cycle. This is the pattern of government spending and taxation prior to the presidential election (e.g., Rogoff 1990; Shi and Svensson 2006). The political budget cycle consists of lower taxes or higher government spending in an election year to stimulate the economy. The budget deficit worsens prior to a presidential election because of the expansionary fiscal policy of the political budget cycle. After the election, the fiscal policy becomes contractionary to reduce inflation caused by preelection fiscal opportunism. Government spending declines or taxes increase following an election. This reduces the government budget deficit after an election.

The political monetary cycle is the pattern of money supply and interest rates in connection with the electoral cycle of the economy (e.g., Abrams and Iossifov 2006; Grier 1989). Higher money supply growth and lower interest rates occur in the election year to boost the economy to increase in-party reelection votes. After the election, a contractionary monetary policy occurs. Money supply growth declines, and interest rates rise to reduce inflation caused by the preelection economic boom.

Electoral Cycle Implications

The electoral cycle distorts the economy and exacerbates swings in the business cycle before and after a presidential election. Rather than steady macroeconomic policy and performance, electoral cycle policies cause excessive macroeconomic demand prior to a presidential election and higher long-run inflation. This policy is followed by contractionary measures and lower aggregate demand and slower economic growth after the election.

Societal economic interests would be served by minimizing the likelihood of the electoral cycle and its economic distortions. A key point is whether the median voter's macroeconomic preference is dynamically inconsistent. The median voter's macroeconomic preference must be inconsistent for the electoral cycle to succeed in increasing in-party reelection voters. Voters must be economically naïve for the electoral cycle to work.

Consequently, reducing the inconsistency of voter preferences reduces the likelihood of an electoral cycle. Several factors promote greater macroeconomic consistency. They include a more-informed public, a vigilant media in providing informed economic commentary, farsighted economic sentiment among opinion leaders in society, and the *watchdog* effect of the out-party.

Dynamic consistency by the median voter does not imply a full grasp of all aspects of the economy. This is unrealistic. Rational ignorance inhibits voters from attaining a total understanding of every facet of the economy (refer to Chapter 5 for a discussion of rational ignorance). In forming a perception of ideal macroeconomic performance, the median citizen relies on the reports and opinions of experts, the media, politicians, political parties, political pundits, think tanks, academics, social critics, and other elites.

Voters partially depend on the commentary of opinion leaders in society as to whether the economy is on the right track or not. Based on the influence of opinion leaders in combination with voters' own perceptions, citizens form attitudes of approval or disapproval on the state of the economy, as well as opinions on the job performance of the president. The rhetoric of opinion makers affects public attitudes. The attributes of opinion makers, such as bias versus farsightedness, affect voter economic awareness. This could either enable or dissuade the president in attempting election-year macroeconomic engineering.

Suppose the net impact of opinion leadership on the economy is naïve or biased. Public attitudes are therefore swayed by opinion makers toward a dynamically inconsistent macroeconomic preference. The external influence of opinion makers causes voter economic preferences to become misinformed. The opinion leader effect induces voter opinions toward unrealistic macroeconomic expectations. The president therefore may be motivated to adopt opportunistic macroeconomic measures to increase reelection votes. In this case, citizens naïvely support an incumbent's opportunistic policy agenda that overheats the economy prior to an election.

Consider the opposite scenario of farsighted opinion-leader sentiment. Suppose opinion-leader farsightedness occurs along with informed economic news reporting and commentary on the dangers of the electoral cycle. The media and opinion leaders recognize and oppose electoral cycle policies because of the economic inefficiency and instability that the PBC effect creates. The actions of the out-party are an additional factor that can inhibit the electoral cycle. The out-party has an important role to play as a political watchdog to inform voters of the macroeconomic distortions caused by in-party electoral cycle policies. The out-party has an interest in opposing in-party macroeconomic opportunism. If macroeconomic overheating succeeds in increasing the in-party presidential reelection vote share, then the out-party presidential vote share declines.

Suppose the out-party effectively warns voters about the economic harm of the electoral cycle. Assume this occurs along with a farsighted opinion leader effect and a vigilant media on the adverse effects of the electoral cycle. Citizens become more aware of the damage that could be caused by reelection-motivated macroeconomic overheating. Voter macroeconomic preferences become more dynamically consistent. Voters form more realistic expectations of the economy. Citizens become more inclined to oppose opportunistic macroeconomic policies out of recognition that the economic gain in an election year is short lived.

The in-party to the White House consequently has no incentive to adopt manipulative macroeconomic measures in an election year because the policy is unlikely to fool voters. Any attempt by the incumbent to alter the economy for political gain backfires. Electoral cycle policies fail. An opportunistic macroeconomic policy causes the in-party presidential reelection vote share to decline rather than increase, given that voters are aware of the manipulation. Because of farsightedness among citizens, electoral cycle macroeconomic policies, if attempted, lead to an increase in votes for the out-party candidate rather than for the in-party in a presidential election. A vigilant media, farsighted opinion leadership, and the out-party watchdog effect reduce the principal–agent problem of a lopsided information disparity on the economy between the president and voters.

Recognition of electoral cycle policies is a relatively straightforward matter in many instances. An electoral cycle is apparent in situations of excessive expansionary policies in an election year when the economy is already at economic potential and full employment. Suppose unemployment is at the natural rate in an election year and expansionary macroeconomic policies are increased. This leads to a short-term decrease in unemployment below the natural rate. The opportunistic macroeconomic policies in an election year could be in the form of tax cuts, increased government spending, or lower interest rates.

This type of scenario is indicative of electoral cycle manipulation. If the media, opinion leaders, and the out-party speak against opportunistic macroeconomic policies, then voters become more aware of the adverse electoral effects. They are more apt to oppose election-year economic engineering. Electoral cycle policies become less likely. The president is compelled to consider the macroeconomic farsightedness of opinion leaders and voters. The president is pressured by a more-informed citizenry to adopt time-consistent macroeconomic policies.

CHAPTER 7

Partisan Political Business Cycle

Introduction

The last chapter focused on the electoral cycle. This chapter examines the partisan cycle (e.g., Hibbs 1982). The president supports policies that attain partisan macroeconomic goals according to the partisan model. Two contrasting partisan effects take place based on which political party occupies the White House. A liberal partisan effect occurs during Democratic incumbencies. A conservative partisan cycle occurs during Republican presidencies.

The president's policy preference deviates from the median voter's most preferred outcome in the partisan model. Presidents adopt the partisan macroeconomic agenda of their core constituencies. This result occurs because of political party dependency on campaign contributions from their core constituencies. To maintain financial funding, political parties embrace policies that satisfy the economic interests of their partisan backers. Partisan supporters reduce their financial contributions if political parties embrace policies that stray from the interests of the core constituencies. The partisan cycle consists of shifts in macroeconomic policy and performance each time the political party in control of the Oval Office changes. This occurs because the liberal and conservative partisan preferences differ from each other.

Macroeconomic Preferences of the Two Main Political Parties

The preferences of the liberal and conservative political parties occur to the left and right of the median voter's most preferred outcome. This partisan divide arises because of the differing macroeconomic preferences of the core constituencies of the two opposing parties. Political candidates embrace policies that satisfy the economic interests of their partisan constituencies, which are their financial backers.

The conservative party tends to align with business and financial interests. These interest groups typically place a high emphasis on maintaining low, stable inflation. The conservative party is relatively inflation averse in its macroeconomic policies. The liberal political party tends to be associated with labor-related unions and organizations. These interest groups generally emphasize low unemployment as a major objective. The liberal political party is relatively unemployment averse in its macroeconomic preference.

Partisan Rhetoric in the Median Voter Model

The median voter model (as discussed in Chapter 5) predicts that the actual policies adopted by the two major political parties tend to converge over time toward the median voter's most preferred outcome. This occurs as a political strategy to increase approval ratings. The political party with the policy nearest to the median voter's preference tends to become the most popular among citizens.

Policy convergence toward the center occurs notwithstanding the opposing partisan rhetoric by the right and left parties. This occurs for two main reasons. First, partisan rhetoric by political parties mobilizes greater political engagement and voting among core partisan constituencies and followers. Active political campaigning by political parties for partisan goals motivates higher voter turnout among partisan supporters. Second, partisan rhetoric by the political parties motivates increased financial support for electoral campaigns. Partisan supporters and interest groups increase donations if their political parties strongly advocate policies in line with their partisan preferences.

After a presidential candidate wins the White House, however, the actual policy ends up being more centrist than suggested by the preelection partisan discourse. The elected president appeals to the median voter to increase approval ratings. In the median voter model, the incumbent deviates from partisan promises and embraces policies that accommodate the median citizen.

Liberal Partisan Cycle

Partisan macroeconomic theory generates different results than the median voter model. Partisan theory maintains that the two political parties not only express opposing partisan rhetoric but embrace different policies. The Democratic party is relatively unemployment averse according to the partisan model. The left party's core constituencies include labor-related organizations and affiliations. High employment is a major economic priority of labor unions and other related interests. Liberal presidencies tend to support expansive fiscal and monetary policies to reduce unemployment.

Political liberals and economic Keynesians support stimulative macroeconomic policies to attain low unemployment. Expansive macroeconomic policies, however, often come at the cost of rising inflation in the long run. According to the partisan model, economic performance during a Democratic presidency typically consists of a pattern of declining or low unemployment in the short run combined with rising inflation in the long run.

Figure 7.1 shows the liberal partisan cycle in the expectational Phillips curve model.

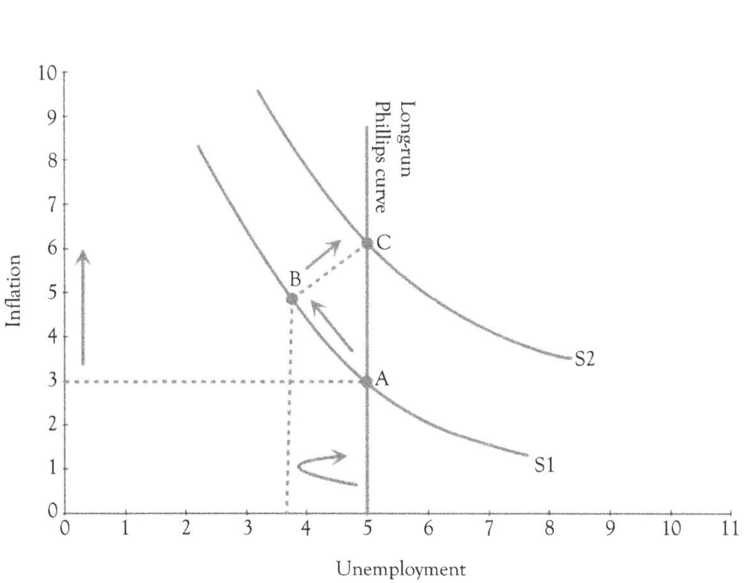

Figure 7.1 Liberal partisan macroeconomic cycle

In Figure 7.1, inflation is measured along the vertical axis, and unemployment is shown along the horizontal axis. The initial equilibrium is point A at the cross between the short-run Phillips curve, S1, and the vertical long-run Phillips curve. Inflation is 3 percent, and unemployment equals the natural rate of 5 percent.

Suppose a Democratic presidency is in power and macroeconomic policy is expansionary. The Democratic incumbency is relatively unemployment averse based on the assumptions of the partisan model. Through expansive stabilization policies, macroeconomic demand rises, and the economy moves upward and to the left along the short-run Phillips curve, S1, from point A to point B.

Unemployment temporarily dips below the natural rate along with rising inflation. Unemployment falls from 5 percent to about 3.75 percent. Unemployment declines as business firms hire more workers to raise production to meet higher macroeconomic demand caused by expansionary policy. Inflation rises because greater macroeconomic demand for goods and services bids up their prices. Inflation rises from 3 to 5 percent.

In the long run of the liberal partisan cycle, the short-run Phillips curve shifts right from S1 to S2, and the economy moves from point B to point C. Unemployment rises and adjusts back to the natural rate through the self-correcting mechanism. Workers adjust their inflationary expectations upward and seek higher wages to compensate for higher product prices caused by higher macroeconomic demand and expansionary policy. Employers respond to higher labor costs by reducing output and jobs. Unemployment rises and returns to the natural rate. Additionally, businesses shift the higher labor costs along to consumers as a further increase in product inflation. Inflation rises from 5 percent to about 6 percent.

In the long run of the liberal partisan cycle, unemployment rises and adjusts back to the natural rate, while inflation rises further. The liberal partisan effect creates only a transitory decline in unemployment below the natural rate. The short-run and long-run outcomes of the liberal partisan cycle are summarized in Table 7.1.

Table 7.1 Liberal partisan cycle

Liberal partisan cycle	Short-run result	Long-run result
Theoretical effects	Increase in macroeconomic demand from expansionary policy; this causes a movement up and along the short-run Phillips curve	Decrease in macroeconomic supply through the self-correction mechanism; the short-run Phillips curve shifts right as worker wages rise to adjust to higher product prices
Inflation	Increases	Further increase
Unemployment	Decreases	Increases to return to the natural rate
RGDP growth	Increases	Decreases to return to the natural RGDP growth rate

Conservative Partisan Cycle

The conservative political party is relatively inflation averse according to the partisan cycle model. The Republican party's core constituencies include pro-business and pro-banking affiliations. Low, stable inflation is a major goal of business and financial interests. Low, stable inflation reduces business and financial risk.

According to the partisan influence model, Republican presidencies support disinflationary policies to maintain low inflation. Disinflationary policies, however, often come at the cost of greater short-term unemployment. Figure 7.2 shows the conservative partisan cycle in the expectational Phillips curve framework.

The starting equilibrium is point C at the cross between the short-run Phillips curve, S2, and the vertical long-run Phillips curve. The economy is at the natural unemployment rate of 5 percent along with inflation of about 6 percent. Suppose the Republican party is in the White House and the macroeconomic policy is contractionary or disinflationary. Conservative presidencies are relatively inflation averse according to the partisan theory. The Republican presidency adopts contractionary stabilization policy and macroeconomic demand declines.

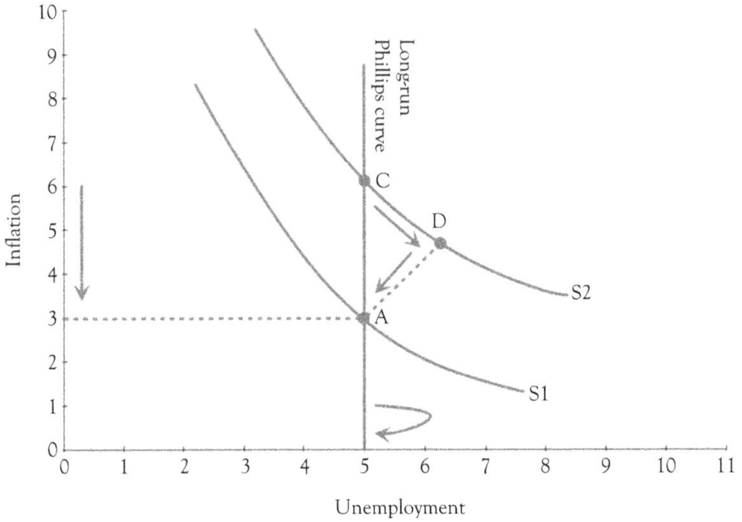

Figure 7.2 *Conservative partisan macroeconomic cycle*

The economy consequently moves from point C to point D along the short-run Phillips curve, S2. Unemployment rises above the natural rate along with lower inflation. Unemployment rises from 5 to 6 percent, while inflation declines from 6 to around 5 percent. For example, a contractionary monetary policy causes interest rates to rise. Consequently, economic investment, consumer spending, and employment decline. Businesses reduce employment and production because of lower macroeconomic demand. Additionally, inflation falls. Lower macroeconomic demand from a contractionary policy compels businesses to reduce product prices to induce consumers to purchase goods.

In the long run, the Phillips curve shifts leftward from S2 to S1 through the self-adjustment mechanism. The economy moves from point D to point A. This takes place as workers reduce their demands for higher wages in reaction to lower product price inflation caused by lower aggregate demand and contractionary policy. The lower labor costs allow firms to decrease product inflation further. Lower real labor costs also enable firms to raise output and jobs. Unemployment therefore decreases and returns to the natural rate, while inflation declines further. Unemployment falls from 6 to 5 percent, while inflation falls from about 5 to 3 percent.

The overall pattern of the conservative partisan cycle consists of lower inflation, rising unemployment, and slower economic growth in the short run. In the long run, unemployment decreases and returns to the natural rate through the self-correcting mechanism of labor market forces. The economic slowdown is alleviated in the long run. The short-run and long-run effects of the conservative partisan cycle are summarized in Table 7.2.

Table 7.2 Conservative partisan cycle

Conservative partisan cycle	Short-run results	Long-run results
Theoretical effects	Decrease in macroeconomic demand from contractionary policy; this causes a movement down and along short-run Phillips curve	Increase in macroeconomic supply through the self-correcting mechanism; the short-run Phillips curve shifts left as real wages decline in response to lower product price inflation
Inflation	Decreases	Further decrease
Unemployment	Increases	Decreases to return to the natural rate
RGDP growth	Decreases	Increases to return to the natural RGDP growth rate

CHAPTER 8

Evidence of Electoral and Partisan Cycles

Introduction

The partisan and electoral cycle effects are a source of macroeconomic instability. The two PBC effects exacerbate the up-and-down swings of the business cycle. This chapter examines the pattern of inflation and unemployment in the U.S. economy for evidence of electoral and partisan effects during Democratic and Republican presidencies across the time frame from 1961 to 2016. As discussed in Chapter 6, the *electoral cycle* refers to incumbent manipulation of the economy prior to an election as a tactic to increase presidential reelection votes (Nordhaus 1975; Nordhaus, Alesina, and Schultze 1989). The partisan effect, as discussed in Chapter 7, refers to incumbent manipulation of stabilization policy to realize partisan macroeconomic goals throughout a presidential term (Alesina and Sachs 1988; Hibbs 1982).

Seven Democratic terms and seven Republican terms occurred from 1961 to 2016. An analysis of inflation and unemployment during this period suggests that liberal partisan cycle effects may have occurred during the Democratic presidencies. The evidence, however, appears mixed regarding PBC effects among the seven Republican presidential terms. Economic performance during five of the seven Republican presidencies seemed to exhibit electoral cycle characteristics. Of the two remaining Republican periods in the White House, one presidential term exhibited a conservative partisan cycle pattern rather than the electoral cycle, while the other Republican presidential term showed no discernible PBC effect.

One possible explanation for the mixed PBC results across Democratic versus Republican incumbencies is that a synthesis of partisan and electoral effects may have occurred during most of the presidencies. A partisan macroeconomic effect may have occurred in the first half of most presidential terms. In the latter part of most presidential terms, macroeconomic policy may have shifted from partisan priority to opportunistic measures. As presidential elections drew closer, administrations may have shifted from partisan economic goals to a policy of unemployment reduction as an attempt to increase presidential reelection votes for the in-party.

Primary and Secondary Electoral and Partisan Effects

This section reviews the predictions, goals, and side effects of the electoral and partisan cycles. The goals are the economic intentions of the PBC policies. The side effects of PBC policies are the adverse macroeconomic consequences that may arise because of the short-run unemployment–inflation trade-off.

Political and economic outcomes affect voter behavior based on rational voter theory. Citizens cast ballots for the candidate or political party that supports policies that most closely align with the voters' most preferred outcomes. In this regard, a substantial body of research shows that a strong economy tends to increase presidential approval and boost presidential reelection votes for the candidate of the incumbent political party. A weak economy diminishes presidential approval and reduces the in-party presidential reelection vote share (Chappell 1983; Fair 1978; Fox 2003, 2009, 2013; Hibbs 2008; Kernell 1978; Smyth, Taylor, and Dua 1999). The relation between the economy and voter sentiment will be discussed in more detail in Chapter 10.

The electoral cycle occurs in two stages. The first phase refers to preelection macroeconomic policy and performance, and the corresponding impact on the presidential reelection vote share. The second phase of the electoral cycle refers to postelection stabilization policy and its macroeconomic effects, and the corresponding impact on presidential approval.

In the preelection period of the electoral cycle, the incumbent embraces an expansionary policy to create an economic boom toward the end of a presidential term. The goal of preelection macroeconomic policy is to reduce unemployment toward the end of the 4-year presidential term. However, because of the short-run inflation–unemployment trade-off, a side effect of rising inflation may develop from opportunistic macroeconomy policy. Much of this inflationary effect is likely to occur after the election because of macroeconomic time lag. An expansionary policy tends to create a more immediate impact on short-term unemployment, which is the intention of the electoral-cycle policy. The long-run economic result of rising inflation tends to take place more gradually, perhaps after a 1-year time lag.

In the postelection phase of the electoral cycle, policy shifts from expansionary to disinflationary. This change in policy is designed to alleviate the inflation caused by the preelection economic over-stimulus. The side effect of postelection disinflationary policy is a possible increase in short-term unemployment. This postelection economic slowdown causes incumbent popularity to decline. Higher unemployment reduces the economic well-being of voters, and consequently presidential approval decreases. Table 8.1 summarizes the effects of the preelection and postelection policies of the electoral cycle.

Table 8.1 Preelection and postelection phases of the electoral cycle

Macroeconomic short-run effects of the electoral cycle	Preelection expansionary macroeconomic policy	Postelection contractionary macroeconomic policy
Goal	Decrease in unemployment and increase in the presidential reelection vote share	Decline in inflation
Side effect	Increase in inflation	Increase in short-run unemployment and a decline in presidential approval

Let us review the predictions and effects of the partisan cycle. According to this model, Republican presidencies are relatively inflation averse in their macroeconomic agenda. This occurs because their core constituencies include business and financial special interests that emphasize the goal of low inflation. Democratic incumbencies are relatively unemployment averse in their macroeconomic preference. This occurs because the liberal party's core constituencies include labor-related interests that emphasize high employment as a major macroeconomic priority. In other words, the conservative party is hawkish on inflation, while the liberal party is dovish on unemployment.

Republican incumbencies adopt a disinflationary policy to attain low or declining inflation throughout a presidential term. This may cause a side effect of rising unemployment. Democratic presidencies adopt an expansionary policy to attain low or declining unemployment throughout a presidential term. This may cause a side effect of rising inflation.

Table 8.2 summarizes the partisan cycle effects for conservative and liberal presidencies.

Table 8.2 Primary and secondary effects of the partisan cycle

Policies and effects	Republican presidencies	Democratic presidencies
Macroeconomic policy	Disinflationary policy	Expansionary policy
Goal	Reduction in inflation	Reduction in unemployment
Side effect	Increase in unemployment	Increase in inflation

Evidence of PBC Effects during Democratic Presidencies

This section examines inflation and unemployment for evidence of PBC effects during Democratic presidencies from 1961 to 2016. Seven Democratic terms occurred during this span. The presidencies include the two terms of Kennedy–Johnson, Carter's term, the first and second terms of Clinton, and the two terms of Obama.

Figure 8.1 shows the inflation–unemployment pattern for each of the Democratic episodes in the White House. Inflation is measured along the vertical axis, while unemployment is depicted next to the horizontal axis. Inflation is based on the consumer price index, while unemployment refers to the percentage of the labor force who are jobless. Both inflation and unemployment come from the Bureau of Labor Statistics (BLS).

Four lines are displayed in Figure 8.1. The lines show the economic patterns during the Democratic periods in the Oval Office. In each of the episodes, the macroeconomic trend is generally consistent with the liberal partisan cycle predictions. Unemployment exhibited a downward trend for most of the years connected with each of the Democratic episodes in

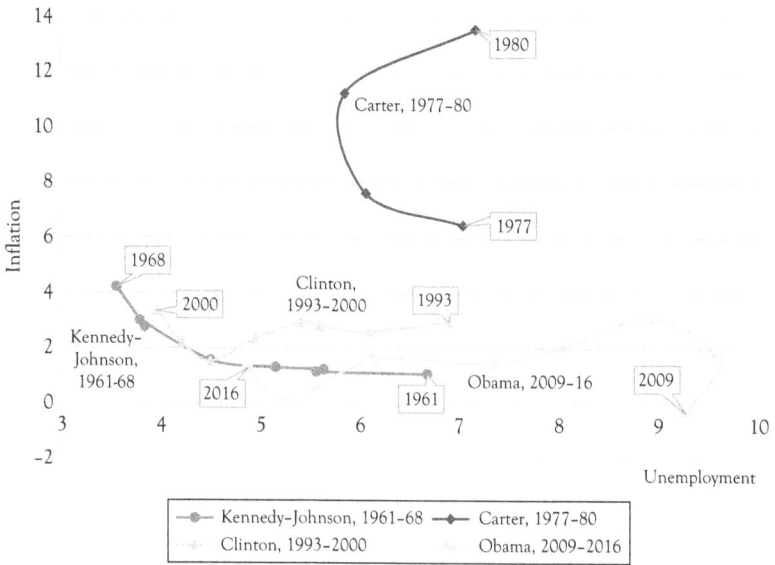

Figure 8.1 *Macroeconomic outcomes during Democratic presidencies*

Source: BLS

the White House. In addition, inflation ended up higher at the end rather than the beginning of each of the Democratic time frames.

The economy during the Kennedy–Johnson period is shown by the line connecting the circle markers (•) in the graph. Across the 8-year interval from 1961 to 1968, the economy experienced declining unemployment and slightly rising inflation. Unemployment gradually fell from 6.7 to 3.6 percent, while inflation rose from 1.1 to 4.2 percent. This result matches the predictions of the liberal partisan cycle.

The economy during the Carter presidency is shown by the line connecting the diamond markers (♦) from 1977 to 1980. The pattern during the first 3 years of the Carter term consisted of declining unemployment and rising inflation. In this period, unemployment fell from 7.1 to 5.9 percent, while inflation rose from 6.5 to 11.2 percent.

The economy, however, exhibited stagflation in the 4th year of the Carter presidency. From 1979 to 1980, inflation continued to climb as predicted by the liberal partisan cycle. Inflation rose from 11.2 to 13.5 percent. The unemployment rate, however, also increased in 1980. Unemployment went up from 5.9 to 7.2 percent. This rise in unemployment contradicts the economic predictions of the liberal partisan cycle. The partisan model expects declining unemployment throughout a liberal presidency.

This stagflationary outcome in 1980 was partially attributable to the spike in oil prices associated with the energy crisis that occurred. The cost of crude oil shot up from $14.95 per barrel in 1978 to a high of $37.42 per barrel in 1980 (http://inflationdata.com/Inflation/Inflation_Rate/Historical_Oil_Prices_Table.asp).

This supply-side oil shock caused macroeconomic supply to decline. This led to a simultaneous increase in inflation and unemployment. The higher energy costs were passed along to buyers in the form of higher product prices. Additionally, business firms reduced production and employment as a cost-cutting device to offset the higher energy expenses. Jimmy Carter lost his 1980 reelection bid partly because of the high stagflation that occurred in the final year of his presidency.

The energy crisis during the latter part of the Carter presidency was an exogenous event that worsened macroeconomic performance from what would otherwise have transpired. Both inflation and unemployment ended up worse than what would have happened had the oil shock not occurred. Because of the exogenous spike in petroleum prices and its stagflationary impact on the economy, the final year of the Carter term (1980) could be excluded from an analysis of PBC effects. If we consider the economy during the first 3 years of the Carter presidency prior to the oil shock, then economic performance exhibited a pattern of rising inflation and decreasing unemployment as predicted by the liberal partisan cycle model.

The economic pattern during the two terms of the Clinton presidency is shown by the line connecting the triangle markers (▲) in Figure 8.1. This was an 8-year period from 1993 to 2000. The economic trend across the Clinton presidency consisted of declining unemployment and gradually rising inflation. Unemployment fell from 6.9 to 4 percent, while inflation rose slightly from 3 to 3.4 percent. Interestingly, the economic pattern during the 8 years of the Clinton presidency closely mirrors the 8-year economic pattern of the Kennedy–Johnson presidencies. The trend of macroeconomic conditions during the Clinton period is consistent with the partisan model predictions for a presidency of the left political party.

The economy during the two terms of the Obama presidency is depicted by the line connecting the square markers (■). Except for 2010, the economy exhibited a gradual decline in unemployment along with an increase in inflation. Unemployment gradually fell from 9.3 to 4.9 percent from 2009 to 2016. Meanwhile, inflation rose from −0.31 to 2.1 percent during the first Obama term and ended up at 1.3 percent in 2016. This economic pattern is generally compatible with the partisan cycle predictions for a liberal incumbency. The one inconsistent unemployment event in the first Obama term was the increase in unemployment in 2010. This, however, was partly because of the negative momentum of the Great Recession of 2007 to 2009.

The macroeconomic outcomes across the four Democratic periods in the White House show a pattern consistent with the predictions of the liberal partisan cycle. The evidence, on the other hand, appears weak for any occurrence of electoral cycle effects during the Democratic incumbencies. The electoral cycle model predicts declining unemployment in election years, which indeed transpired for most of the Democratic presidencies. However, a general pattern of declining unemployment and rising inflation occurred for most of the years associated with each of the Democratic spans in the Oval Office, not just prior to elections. These economic results are more compatible with the liberal partisan cycle than the electoral cycle.

Evidence of PBC Effects during Republican Presidencies

Let us examine the economy for evidence of partisan and electoral cycle effects during the Republican administrations from 1961 to 2016. Seven Republican terms occurred in this interval. The presidencies are Nixon, Nixon–Ford, Reagan's first and second terms, G.H. Bush, and the two terms of G.W. Bush. Figure 8.2 shows the pattern of inflation and unemployment during the 8-year span from 1969 to 1976 corresponding to the two presidential terms of Nixon and Nixon–Ford.

The line connecting the points denotes the economic events of the Nixon–Ford incumbencies. A clockwise spiral pattern occurred for macroeconomic performance during this period. This is generally consistent

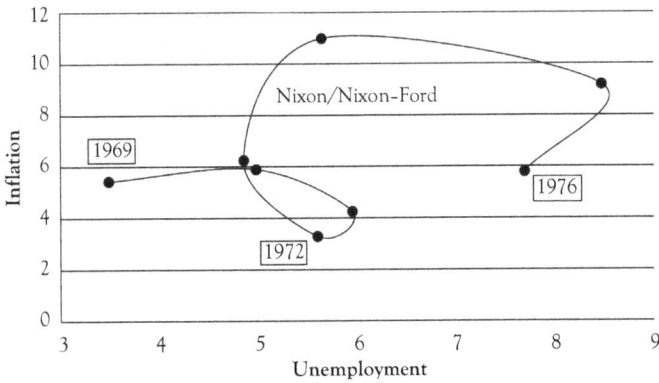

Figure 8.2 Macroeconomic performance during the Nixon–Ford presidencies

Source: BLS

with the electoral cycle predictions. Disinflationary economic contractions occurred during the mid-part of each of the two terms, followed by macroeconomic recoveries in the election years, and rising inflation after the elections.

As predicted by the electoral cycle, the 1972 election-year economic recovery provided a boost to the presidential reelection vote share for the Republican Party, and Nixon easily won a second term in office. Following the 1972 vote, inflation rose during 1973 to 1974. This inflationary outcome was partly because of the preelection opportunistic macroeconomic policy. Part of this inflationary pressure was also due to an increase in oil prices associated with the 1973 Oil Embargo.

This postelection inflation problem was addressed by a contractionary macroeconomic policy after the 1972 vote. This disinflationary policy came at the economic cost of a 14-month recession from November 1973 to March 1975. Economic performance did improve somewhat by the time of the 1976 presidential vote. Both unemployment and inflation declined in that election year as predicted by the electoral cycle. In this instance, the recovering economy in an election year was not substantial enough for the in-party to retain the White House. Instead, the Democratic challenger, Jimmy Carter, defeated the Republican incumbent, Gerald Ford, in the 1976 vote. After this election, inflation increased as predicted by the electoral cycle model. Although not shown in Figure 8.2, inflation rose from 5.8 percent in 1976 to 6.5 percent in 1977.

In summary, disinflationary macroeconomic slowdowns occurred during the middle of the Nixon and Nixon–Ford terms, followed by pre-election economic expansions and postelection rising inflation. These results are consistent with the electoral cycle hypothesis.

Let us consider the economy during the Reagan era from 1981 to 1988. Figure 8.3 illustrates the inflation–unemployment pattern for this time frame.

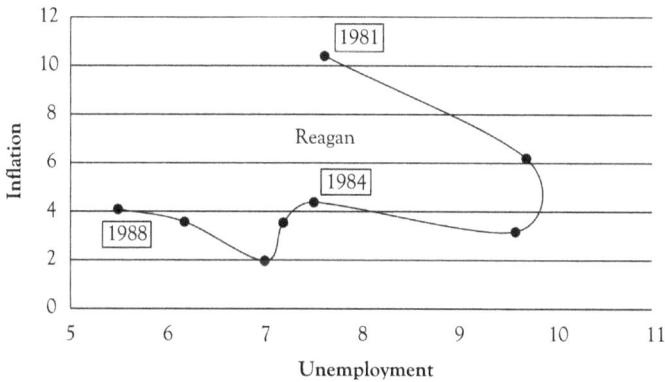

Figure 8.3 Macroeconomic performance during the Reagan administration

Source: BLS

The line connecting the points in the chart denotes the economy across the two terms of the Reagan White House. This macroeconomic pattern is compatible with several electoral cycle predictions. Disinflation occurred during the middle part of each of the two terms. This was followed by a substantial improvement in unemployment in the latter part of each of the two Reagan terms prior to the presidential elections. The Republican Party consequently won reelection to the White House at the end of each of the two Reagan terms, partly because of the election-year economic booms.

The first Reagan term was from 1981 to 1984. A disinflationary recession arose in the first half of this term. This economic slowdown from 1981 to 1982 was caused by the contractionary monetary policy that was adopted to cure the high inflation inherited from the 1970s. This inflation was caused by economic overheating during the Carter presidency and from high oil prices associated with the two energy crises of the 1970s. By 1983, inflation had subsided dramatically because of the tight monetary policy. The fall in inflation was also partially due to a decrease in oil prices beginning in the early 1980s. By the time of the 1984 vote, the monetary policy had shifted from contractionary to expansionary as predicted by the electoral cycle. Consequently, unemployment fell dramatically, while inflation rose slightly in 1984. Reagan was subsequently reelected to the White House mainly because of the recovering economy in the election year.

The second Reagan term was from 1985 and 1988. The electoral cycle effect in this period is less clear than the earlier Reagan term. However, the macroeconomic conditions in the second Reagan term are consistent with some of the predictions of the electoral cycle. The economy experienced disinflation during the first part of the second Reagan term from 1985 to 1986 as predicted by the electoral cycle. Inflation fell substantially, while unemployment decreased slightly. The low oil prices of the 1980s was a favorable supply-side factor that contributed to lower inflation and unemployment. In the latter part of the second Reagan term, the economy exhibited a more expansionary turn as predicted by the electoral cycle. Unemployment declined markedly, while inflation rose slightly from 1986 to 1988. The Republican Party was subsequently reelected to the White House in the 1988 vote, partly because of the low-unemployment economy. G.H. Bush (R) defeated Michael Dukakis (D) in that election.

The G.H. Bush presidency was from 1989 to 1992. Unlike the previous Republican administrations, the macroeconomic pattern in this period was compatible with the conservative partisan cycle rather than the electoral cycle. During most of the G.H. Bush presidency, the economy exhibited a trend of declining inflation and rising unemployment. Figure 8.4 shows this pattern.

The line connecting the points in the chart denotes economic outcomes across the G.H. Bush presidency. In the 4-year time span from 1989 to 1992, inflation fell from 4.8 to 3.05 percent, while unemployment rose from 5.3 to 7.5 percent. These results are consistent with the

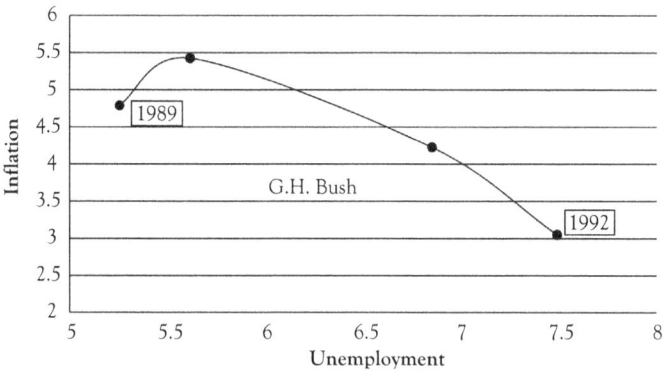

Figure 8.4 *Macroeconomic performance during G.H. Bush presidency*

Source: BLS

partisan cycle predictions for a presidency of the conservative political party. The high unemployment rate prior to the presidential vote was a major factor in the 1992 reelection defeat of G.H. Bush.

The G.W. Bush presidency was from 2001 to 2008. Figure 8.5 shows the economic outcomes across the two terms of G.W. Bush. The line connecting the points indicates the economic pattern. The economic trend during the first term is compatible with some of the predictions of the electoral cycle. During the first part of the first G.W. Bush term, a

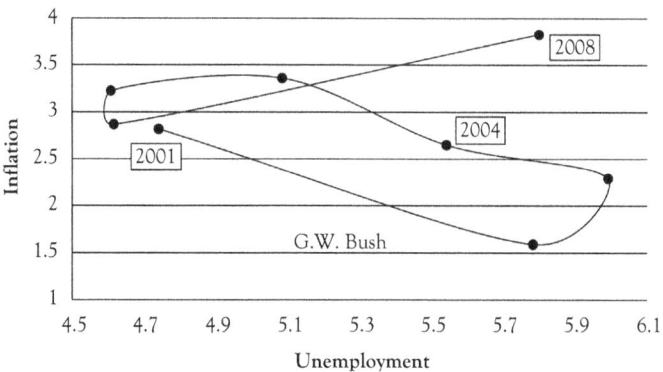

Figure 8.5 *Macroeconomic performance during G.W. Bush presidency*

Source: BLS

contractionary macroeconomic effect occurred. Inflation fell, while unemployment increased. This economic contraction was followed by an expansionary turn in macroeconomic performance in the election year of 2004, wherein unemployment fell, while inflation increased. G.W. Bush was subsequently reelected to the Oval Office, partly because of the decline in unemployment in the election year.

The second term of the G.W. Bush presidency was from 2005 to 2008. The economic pattern in this period does not match the predictions of either the conservative partisan cycle or the electoral cycle. The economy experienced rising inflation throughout the second term of the G.W. Bush presidency. Unemployment, on the other hand, fell during the first half of the second term but then rose dramatically by the time of the 2008 presidential vote. This spike in unemployment marked the beginning of the Great Recession of 2008 to 2009. The Republican Party lost the 2008 presidential election partly because of the worsening economic performance.

Summary of PBC Effects across Political Parties and Presidencies

The pattern of inflation and unemployment from 1961 to 2016 exhibited differing PBC characteristics for Democratic versus Republican incumbencies. Liberal partisan cycle effects occurred during the seven Democratic presidencies. In contrast, five of the seven Republican terms exhibited electoral cycle effects. These administrations were Nixon, Nixon–Ford, the first and second Reagan terms, and the first G.W. Bush term.

Two of the seven Republican terms did not exhibit electoral cycle effects. These presidencies were G.H. Bush and the second G.W. Bush term. The economy during the G.H. Bush presidency exhibited a conservative partisan cycle effect. And the economy during the second term of G.W. Bush was not compatible with either the partisan cycle or the electoral cycle.

Table 8.3 summarizes the economic patterns and the PBC effects for the Republican and Democratic presidencies.

Table 8.3 PBC effects between 1961 and 2016

Presidential term	Macroeconomic pattern	PBC effect
Kennedy–Johnson (D) 1961–1964	Falling unemployment and rising inflation	Liberal partisan cycle
Johnson (D) 1965–1968	Falling unemployment and rising inflation	Liberal partisan cycle
Nixon (R) 1969–1972	Economic contraction followed by recovery in the election year	Electoral cycle
Nixon–Ford (R) 1973–1976	Economic contraction followed by recovery in the election year	Electoral cycle
Carter (D) 1977–1980	Falling unemployment and rising inflation (excluding 1980 oil shock)	Liberal partisan cycle
Reagan first term (R) 1981–1984	Economic contraction followed by recovery in the election year	Electoral cycle
Reagan second term (R) 1985–1988	Disinflation followed by economic expansion	Electoral cycle
G.H. Bush (R) 1989–1992	Declining inflation and rising unemployment	Conservative partisan cycle
Clinton first term (D) 1993–1996	Falling unemployment and slightly rising inflation	Liberal partisan cycle
Clinton second term (D) 1997–2000	Falling unemployment and slightly rising inflation	Liberal partisan cycle
G.W. Bush first term (R) 2001–2004	Economic contraction followed by recovery in the election year	Electoral cycle
G.W. Bush second term (R) 2005–2008	Falling unemployment and then rising unemployment	No discernible PBC effect
Obama first and second terms (D), 2009–2016	Large decline in unemployment and generally stable low inflation	Liberal partisan cycle

Synthesis of PBC Effects

A synthesis of the two PBC effects is one way to reconcile the different macroeconomic patterns between the two political parties. The PBC synthesis occurs in two stages. Partisan macroeconomic performance occurs in the first part of a presidential term. Administrations embrace policies to attain the partisan macroeconomic goals of their core constituencies. Partisan economic performance is followed by a shift to opportunistic policies in the latter part of a presidential term. This occurs as a political strategy to increase the in-party presidential reelection vote share. Consequently, the PBC synthesis for Democratic presidencies resembles the liberal partisan cycle, while the PBC synthesis for Republican incumbencies resembles the electoral cycle.

In Republican presidencies, the PBS synthesis suggests that disinflation occurs in the first half of a presidential term followed by an economic expansion in the latter part of the term. Conservative presidencies pursue the partisan goal of low inflation during the first part of a 4-year presidency. In the latter part of a conservative presidential term, macroeconomic policy shifts from partisan objectives to expansionary measures. This reduces unemployment as an attempt to increase the presidential reelection vote share.

For Democratic incumbencies, the PBC synthesis resembles the liberal partisan cycle of unemployment aversion throughout a presidential term. A left-party incumbency adopts expansionary measures in the first part of a term based on the liberal objective of unemployment aversion. During the second part of the term, the liberal administration maintains expansionary policies based on the left agenda of unemployment aversion combined with electoral ambition to reduce unemployment to improve the presidential reelection vote share. Table 8.4 summarizes the PBC synthesis for Republican versus Democratic presidencies.

Table 8.4 Partisan–electoral PBC synthesis

Synthesis of partisan and electoral effects	Democratic presidencies	Republican presidencies
A partisan policy during the first part of a term	An expansionary policy based on the liberal preference of relative unemployment aversion	A contractionary policy based on the conservative preference of relative inflation aversion
An opportunistic policy during the second part of a term	An expansionary policy to reduce unemployment in order to increase presidential reelection votes	An expansionary policy to reduce unemployment in order to increase presidential reelection votes

CHAPTER 9

Other Political Business Cycle Considerations

Chapters 6, 7, and 8 examined some of the theoretical and empirical characteristics of the electoral and partisan PBC effects. This chapter looks at some additional issues regarding political influence on macroeconomic policy and the economy. We will consider in more detail the main assumptions of the electoral and partisan effects. We will also discuss macroeconomic uncertainty and its influence on election outcomes. Finally, we will examine the subject of central bank independence and the related topic of a monetary policy rule.

Main Assumptions of the Electoral and Partisan Effects

Three key assumptions underlie the electoral and partisan cycle effects:

- *President's Policy Preference:* The partisan and electoral effects assume that the president's macroeconomic preference focuses on partisan goals or reelection ambition.
- *Presidential Power:* The partisan and electoral effects assume that the president has power to determine macroeconomic policy.
- *Macroeconomic Predictability:* The partisan and electoral effects assume that the impact of stabilization policy on the economy is accurate and predictable.

Let us consider each of these assumptions.

President's Policy Preference

The president's policy preference focuses either on partisan economic goals or on increasing reelection votes according to the electoral and partisan effects. For example, if the median voter's macroeconomic preference is dynamically inconsistent, then the president might support an opportunistic policy as an attempt to gain reelection.

The president, on the other hand, could prefer a different economic strategy, even if opportunistic policies would be effective in increasing reelection votes. Various factors can impact a president's policy preference. Ethical considerations, for example, may cause an incumbent to reject opportunistic policies. The electoral cycle effect is Machiavellian in nature. The ends justify the means. To increase reelection votes, citizens are misled into accepting fleeting economic gains that occur at the expense of higher postelection inflation, which may be followed by a disinflationary recession.

Other concerns could also cause an incumbent not to pursue PBC policies. The president may have a different macroeconomic agenda besides partisan priority or reelection ambition. An administration might choose to concentrate on issues such as reducing government debt, tax reform, health care, poverty alleviation, international trade, education, national defense, or environmentalism. The president, however, must be able to resist PBC political pressures to pursue a distinct macroeconomic program. Many motivations likely affect the economic agenda of a presidential administration, such as political party platform, reelection strategies, and fulfillment of campaign promises.

President's Influence on Macroeconomic Policy

The next issue is the president's power to influence the macroeconomic policy. The incumbent does not fully determine the macroeconomic policy. The president does not completely decide the fiscal policy and has only an indirect influence on the monetary policy. The president is therefore not always able to attain the desired macroeconomic agenda.

Monetary policy is directly determined by the Federal Reserve and not by the executive branch. To reduce undue political influence, the Fed has been set up as an independent institution. The Fed is not required to adhere to the economic preferences of the president or the Congress. The incumbent, however, may indirectly affect the Fed through the presidential appointment of the Fed Chairperson. The Fed Chair, for instance, may choose to support the incumbent's macroeconomic agenda because of loyalty to the president or out of ambition to be reappointed as Fed Chair.

Additionally, fiscal policy is not under full control of the presidency. Fiscal policy is determined by the political compromise between the president and the Congress. Fiscal policy occurs mainly through the federal budget process. The fiscal policy process also involves the partisan economic platforms of the right and left political parties and their influence on the president and the Congress.

The president's impact on fiscal policy is likely to be substantial in a unified government. A unified government occurs if one political party controls both the executive and legislative branches. This takes place if the in-party to the White House possesses a majority of seats in both the Senate and House. The number of in-party legislators is greater than the number of out-party legislators in a unified government. The in-party legislators can outvote the out-party legislators. In-party legislators in the House and Senate are likely to support the president's budget proposal and other fiscal policy initiatives by the administration. The president has a relatively strong sway over the level and distribution of taxes and government expenditures in a unified government.

A presidential administration is more likely to achieve its fiscal policy agenda in a unified government than a divided government. A divided government occurs if one party controls the presidency while the opposing party has a majority of the seats in Congress. A divided government also occurs if one party has a majority of seats in the House of Representatives, while the opposing party has a majority of seats in the Senate.

Partisan gridlock may occur regarding fiscal policy in a divided government. The out-party in control of Congress may oppose the fiscal policy program of the in-party in control of the Oval Office. The out-party legislators outnumber the in-party legislators in a divided government. The out-party legislators are likely to oppose the president's budget proposal. The in-party legislators are likely to support the president's budget plan. The out-party legislators, however, can outvote the in-party legisla-tors. The president consequently has weaker sway over fiscal policy in a divided government than a unified government. If partisan gridlock oc-curs, neither political party is likely to achieve their preferred fiscal policy. Both parties must compromise on taxes and government spending. This process of finding compromise on taxes and government spending may be difficult because the political left and political right often clash on the role and size of government in the economy. In a worst-case scenario, a government shutdown could occur until compromise is reached.

Another partisan-related effect is that the out-party may choose to oppose fiscal policy initiatives by the president that could boost the econ-omy and improve reelection chances for the in-party. A strong economy leads to an increase in presidential and congressional votes for the in-party and a decrease in votes for out-party candidates. Consequently, the out-party may cynically hope for a weak economy prior to a presidential election or a midterm election. A slow economy in an election year tends to boost presidential and congressional votes for out-party candidates and reduce votes for in-party candidates.

Macroeconomic Unpredictability and the Policy Lag Effect

A further matter is the partial unpredictability of the economy in reaction to policy. RGDP, unemployment, and inflation do not always respond to macroeconomic policy in terms of magnitude or timing as intended. Suppose the president manipulates policy for an intended electoral cycle effect. Opportunistic policy does not guarantee the economy will react precisely as predicted. The macroeconomy does not always respond in the time frame nor to the extent that is planned.

An attempt by the incumbent to orchestrate an electoral effect (or a partisan effect) could be thwarted by uncertainty and unpredictabil-ity on the impact of policy on the economy. Fine-tuning of the econ-omy through policy to create a PBC effect may be difficult to achieve. The macroeconomic policy could mistakenly overshoot or undershoot a desired electoral cycle effect. If opportunistic policy is too weak, the economy will not expand sufficiently prior to the election as planned by the incumbent. The administration, consequently, will not achieve its goal of a strong pre-election economic stimulus. The in-party could consequently lose reelection to the White House because of weaker than anticipated economic performance. Alternatively, if opportunistic policy is too strong, then inflationary overheating develops prior to the presidential vote, which hurts reelection chances.

Besides uncertainty on the effects of macroeconomic policy, the second issue regarding unpredictability is policy timing. A time lag occurs between the implementation of policy and its subsequent influence on the economy. Because of policy lag uncertainty, policy could be inaccurately timed. Policy may impact the economy too quickly or too slowly. If the impact of an electoral-cycle policy occurs too rapidly, rising inflation develops prior to the election rather than afterward as intended. This unintended preelection inflation jeopardizes reelection ambitions for the in-party.

Alternatively, opportunistic policy may impact the economy more slowly than predicted. The economic boom consequently occurs after the election rather than before. The in-party could lose reelection because of the lagged response of the economy to expansionary measures. The economy during the G.H. Bush presidency may have been an instance of the policy lag effect in connection with the 1992 presidential election. The economy throughout the G.H. Bush presidency of 1989 to 1992 exhibited a conservative partisan cycle pattern of disinflation and rising unemployment. This partisan macroeconomic effect was in contrast to the electoral cycle pattern that seemed to occur for most other Republican terms during the post-1960 time frame (see Chapter 8 for a discussion).

Monetary policy during the G.H. Bush term, however, became expansionary prior to the 1992 presidential vote, perhaps as an attempt to create a preelection economic expansion. Monetary policy turned expansionary toward the end of the G.H. Bush term as predicted by the electoral cycle. M1 money supply growth was low at a disinflationary rate of 3.6 percent during 1989 to 1990. Money supply growth then increased to 6 percent in 1991, and to an expansionary rate of 12.4 percent in the election year of 1992 (Federal Reserve Economic Data). This shift from a disinflationary policy to an expansionary policy toward the end of the G.H. Bush term, however, did not yield lower unemployment until after the 1992 presidential election, rather than prior to the vote as expected by the electoral cycle. Unemployment remained high at 7.8 percent in 1992. In 1993, however, after the election, unemployment fell to as low as 6.5 percent (Bureau of Labor Statistics).

The expansionary monetary policy, in other words, may have had a slower than expected impact on the economy toward the end of the G.H. Bush term. The economy may have exhibited a failed electoral cycle during the G.H. Bush presidency. The weak economy in the election year of 1992 was a major cause for the reelection defeat of G.H. Bush. If unemployment had declined prior to the 1992 vote rather than afterward, G.H. Bush would probably have received a higher presidential reelection vote share.

Macroeconomic Shocks and Macroeconomic Uncertainty

Exogenous shocks are major external events that alter economic performance from its previous pattern. Shocks are an inevitable and periodic characteristic of the economy and a source of uncertainty. Exogenous shocks can either cancel out or amplify macroeconomic policies, including actions based on reelection ambition or partisan priorities. Economic shocks may also be beneficial or detrimental. A beneficial shock improves the economy and likely boosts presidential approval and the presidential reelection vote share. An adverse shock worsens the economy. This weakens presidential approval and reduces the presidential reelection vote share for the in-party.

Exogenous shocks may occur on the supply side as well as the demand side of the economy. Two types of supply-side shocks are commercial technology and resource costs, especially energy prices. For example, a dramatic and sustained change in oil prices could either exacerbate or negate a PBC effect. A substantial decline in oil prices prior to a presidential election could cause both inflation and unemployment to fall as well as economic growth to expand. This magnifies an electoral cycle effect. The political result of this positive supply-side shock is likely to be an increase in presidential approval and an increase presidential reelection votes.

An instance of this type of supply-side effect was the decline in oil prices during the early 1980s. This positive supply-side effect strengthened the economy toward the end of Reagan's first term in the White

House. Both inflation and unemployment fell. This was a positive factor in Reagan's reelection victory in 1984. A similar supply-side effect was the decline in oil prices prior to the 2004 presidential vote. This led to disinflation in the election year. This may have been a contributing factor in G.W. Bush's reelection victory.

Conversely, a substantial rise in oil prices can cause both inflation and unemployment to worsen. If this happens prior to a presidential election, then the reelection votes for the in-party presidential candidate will probably decline. An example of this effect was the energy shock on the 1980 presidential election. The Oil Crisis of 1979 to 1980 occurred toward the end of the Carter term. This shock caused the economy to diverge from its previous liberal partisan cycle pattern of declining unemployment (see Chapter 8). Instead, stagflation occurred because of the oil crisis. Both unemployment and inflation rose prior to the 1980 vote. This was a major factor in the presidential reelection defeat of Jimmy Carter.

Besides supply-side shocks, macroeconomic shocks can occur on the demand side. An important demand-side factor is the periodic occurrence of large private debt bubbles. An example of a debt bubble crisis was the real-estate and financial crash that lead to the Great Recession prior to the 2008 presidential election. The Great Recession began in the final year of the G.W. Bush presidency. In 2006 and 2007 prior to the financial crisis and the Great Recession, a pattern of slight disinflation arose. This economic effect is consistent with either the electoral cycle or a conservative partisan cycle (see Chapter 8 for a discussion). This macroeconomic pattern, however, was interrupted in 2008 by the shock of the financial crisis and the Great Recession. Consequently, both inflation and unemployment increased. This stagflationary outcome was a key factor in the Republican loss of the White House in the 2008 presidential election.

Macroeconomic Uncertainty and Presidential Reelection Vulnerability

Economic events obviously fluctuate across presidencies. This happens partly because of the complex relationship and interaction among the macroeconomic policymakers and the various considerations that weigh on policy decisions. The policymakers are the president, the Congress, the Fed, and the indirect influence of the liberal and conservative political parties. These policymakers interact with one another to influence fiscal and monetary policies.

The process of macroeconomic policy and its effect on the business cycle do not follow one simple pattern over time across all administrations. In Chapter 8, we examine business cycle data and found evidence for differing PBC effects across Republican versus Democratic presidencies. Different policymakers have different macroeconomic priorities at different times. Policymakers also face differing economic circumstances at different times, such as periodic episodes of recession versus other periods of high inflation. These fluctuating economic circumstances lead to different macroeconomic policies across different incumbencies. Additionally, stabilization policy lag, exogenous economic shocks, and various macroeconomic uncertainties and rigidities create unpredictability in the business cycle.

The reelection prospects of a president are vulnerable to economic uncertainty. An incumbent's chance of reelection is partly dependent on the fortune or misfortune of a partially unpredictable economy. The president may adopt policies based on reelection ambition, partisan priorities, or other objectives. The fickleness of the economy, however, partially jeopardizes the realization of these goals.

The unpredictability of the ups and downs of the business cycle can impact whether the economy is strong or weak on election eve. The good luck or bad luck of the business cycle influences presidential and congressional election outcomes. The fortune or misfortune of the economy in an election year affects which candidate and political party win and who lose in presidential and congressional elections.

The incumbent is held accountable to voters in elections based on how well the economy performs. This accountability occurs regardless of whether the president is responsible for the economic events. The incumbent is rewarded with a high reelection vote share if a strong economy occurs. This electoral outcome tends to take place irrespective of whether the administration creates the favorable macroeconomic outcomes or not. An incumbent might be reelected because of a strong economy that is unrelated to the president's policies. A president tends to receive a low reelection vote share if a weak economy occurs. This tends to take place regardless of whether the administration's policies cause the poor economic performance or not. An incumbent might lose reelection because of a weak economy that is beyond the control of the administration to prevent.

Central Bank Independence?

The Federal Reserve System is an independent government entity. The institution is set up to be insulated from excessive special interest influence and undue political and partisan pressures from the president and the Congress. The independent nature of the central bank is based on the concept that monetary policy should be protected from political pressures that could be unstable and inefficient. The monetary policy decision-making process is designed to be autonomous and based on economic criteria rather than shifting political winds. In the absence of an independent Fed, Congressional and presidential politics could influence the central bank to adopt monetary measures based on popularity, special interests, partisanship, or political expediency rather than economic considerations.

Macroeconomic circumstances, for example, may sometimes require unpopular actions by the monetary authority. A tight monetary policy, for example, is often necessary to resolve high inflation. Disinflation from tight policy can cause a temporary recession because of the short-run inflation–unemployment trade-off. While effective at reducing inflation, restrictive monetary measures can be controversial among voters and interest groups because of the negative side effect of an economic slowdown. Opposition to central bank policy can consequently develop. This political discontentment could influence monetary policy decisions in the absence of an independent Fed. The central bank might be politically pressed to adopt an expansionary policy to alleviate the economic slowdown, but with the long-term consequence of an even further rise in inflation.

Three Elements of Central Bank Independence

The independent nature of the Fed includes three elements:

1. The Fed earns its income rather than being dependent on the Congress for funding.

2. The Fed chair and Board of Governors are appointed to serve terms that extend across multiple presidencies.
3. Monetary policy does not require approval from the Congress or the president.

The Fed is financially insulated from partisan and electoral pressures of the executive and legislative branches. The Fed earns its own income rather than being reliant on the Congress for funding through the federal budget. The central bank is not subject to the budgetary process of political interaction among the Congress, the presidency, and the political parties. The Fed does not depend on taxes to finance its operations and activities. Instead, the Fed earns income through bank fees, interest payments, and other charges for various services it provides to member banks of the Federal Reserve System. The central bank thus maintains financial freedom from the presidency and the Congress. If the Congress could determine the central bank's budget, then the Fed might be pressured to acquiesce to Congressional preferences on monetary policy and banking regulations.

Besides financial independence, a second aspect of central bank independence is the appointment of Fed officials. The president appoints the seven members of the board of governors of the Fed. Each member serves a nonrenewable, staggered 14-year term that spans across multiple presidential administrations. One new board member is appointed every 2 years to replace a retiring member. This creates the staggered effect.

The president also appoints the chair and vice-chair of the board of governors. These appointments consist of renewable 4-year terms. The chair, vice-chair, and other members of the Board of Governors, combined with 5 of the 12 Federal Reserve District Bank Presidents, constitute the Federal Open Market Committee (FOMC). The FOMC determines monetary policy and its influence on money supply and interest rates. The appointed Fed chairperson is particularly important in the monetary policy process. The Fed chair sets the monetary policy agenda for the FOMC.

Because of the appointment mechanism of Fed officials, the actions of the central bank are not directly subject to democratic elections. Electoral determination of Fed officials could conceivably compromise the economic integrity of monetary policy. If central bank policymakers were accountable through periodic elections, then the central bank might decide to adopt policies based on popularity or political expediency rather than economic criteria that may sometimes be unpopular but necessary (such as a tight policy to alleviate high inflation that could cause an unpopular temporary recession).

The third main element of central bank independence is that monetary policy does not involve approval from the president or the Congress. Elected politicians, however, have a strong interest in Fed actions because of its impact on the economy. The state of the economy affects voter well-being and therefore election outcomes. Consequently, elected officials often express their viewpoints about the Fed and monetary policy. However, neither the executive nor legislative branches can mandate the direction of monetary policy because of the independence of the central bank.

Fed Independence Is Partial

The monetary authority is not completely immune from political pressures associated with special interests, voters, the Congress, and the presidency. One interest group that may influence central bank policy is the financial industry. One criticism of the Fed is that banking and financial interests have excessive impact on central bank decisions. The Fed might adopt policies that benefit financial institutions more than the overall economy. Additionally, many members of the Board of Governors of the Fed have career connections to banking and financial institutions. These interconnections can create a conflict of interest.

The central bank could be pressured to adopt monetary and regulatory policies that increase the profitability of Wall Street to the detriment of the total economy. In a worst-case scenario, a boom-and-bust economic cycle could arise that benefits financial markets and financial institutions. The Fed, for example, might adopt excessively expansive monetary measures and lax banking regulations that boost the short-term profitability of financial firms in the form of a booming stock market and high returns on risky financial loans and bonds. Weak financial regulations could enable excessive unsafe loans combined with rapid money supply growth that keeps interest rates too low for too long.

This type of scenario may have played out with the financial crisis of 2007 to 2008 and the corresponding Great Recession of 2007 to 2009. Prior to this crisis, a financial bubble arose in the form of high private debt from risky mortgage loans combined with low interest rates and stock market speculation. This bubble eventually burst through risky loan defaults and a stock market crash. The economy subsequently sunk into a severe recession. In the end, big banks and financial institutions were bailed out by the government.

Besides the influence of the financial industry, the Fed is partially subject to presidential and Congressional pressures. The Fed chair, for example, must testify before the Congress on a periodic basis regarding monetary policy and the state of the economy. The Fed chair is not compelled to adhere to the recommendations of legislators in Congressional hearings. The central bank, however, may experience political pressure to alter policy to accommodate Congressional sentiment. Congress, for instance, could threaten to pass laws that interfere with monetary policy. In an extreme circumstance, the Congress could threaten impeachment of the Fed chair if legislators considered central bank policies to be irresponsible.

Congressional influence on the central bank could be either beneficial or harmful. If Congressional pressure on the Fed is based on shifting and inefficient politics and partisanship, then Congressional involvement with the monetary authority can become detrimental. If, however, Congressional monitoring of central bank activity is based on reasonable analysis, then legislative oversight of the Fed is beneficial safeguard. Besides Congressional pressure on the central bank, the greatest source of executive branch influence is the presidential appointment of the chair of the central bank. The president is likely to appoint a Fed chair who embraces the same macroeconomic agenda as the administration. Out of loyalty, the Fed chair may also feel pressure to adopt a monetary policy consistent with the economic preferences of the president.

Executive branch influence on the central bank could be further exacerbated if the Fed chair seeks reappointment. In hopes of reappointment to the position, the Fed chair may enact monetary policies in line with the administration's economic program. On the other hand, the Fed chair and the FOMC might choose to adopt monetary policy that conflicts with the administration's priorities. In this case, the president may decide not to re-appoint the Fed chair and instead assign a different member of the Board of Governors to the position. Based on these executive branch pressures on the central bank, the electoral and partisan PBC effects assume that monetary policy tends to follow the president's preference.

Besides financial interests and presidential and Congressional pressures, the Fed is scrutinized by the media, various other special interests, opinion leaders, political parties, and the public. Any individual or group may criticize the central bank if monetary policy is perceived as too expansionary or too contractionary, or if banking regulations are considered too weak or too restrictive. Likewise, any group or person may praise the Fed's actions if monetary policy and financial regulations are viewed as effective. Various political influences likely exert some impact on the central bank. The magnitude of these external political pressures on monetary policy is difficult to calculate.

The net impact of outside political forces on central bank policy could be either beneficial or detrimental based on the farsightedness or short-sightedness of the various pressures. If the impact of politics on the Fed is shortsighted, then monetary policy could become too contractionary or too expansionary. External political influence on the Fed could also be beneficial. From the Congressional and presidential perspectives, the central bank should consider their sentiments, which reflect the attitudes of voters, political parties, and interest groups. If the macroeconomic perceptions of the Congress and the administration are enlightened and farsighted, then their pressure on monetary policy is helpful. Enlightened political pressures could influence the monetary authority to have a more responsive policy.

The independent nature of the Fed could have either a positive or negative overall effect. Central bank independence is effective if the Fed adopts efficient monetary policy based on economic criteria as intended. Central bank independence, however, could conceivably become detrimental. An independent Fed is potentially harmful if the central bank is not held accountable for mismanagement of monetary policy decisions should they occur. Central bank independence could lead to policy actions that are out of touch with societal economic needs. The central bank might pursue short-term financial interests to the detriment of the overall economy. Excessive banking deregulations or overly expansive monetary policies could lead to financial bubbles that bulge and then burst.

Discretionary Monetary Policy versus a Monetary Policy Rule

Macroeconomic policy occurs according to the discretionary judgment of the policymakers. The discretionary interaction between the president and the Congress determines fiscal policy. The discretionary interaction between the Fed chair and the other FOMC members determines monetary policy. Additionally, political pressure from voters, political parties, the media, and interest groups likely has some indirect influence on the discretionary actions of the fiscal and monetary policymakers.

For example, the president as well as Congressional legislators may have difficulty gaining reelection if their policies do not reflect citizen sentiment on the economy. Additionally, elected officials may have difficulty obtaining sufficient financial backing for election campaigns if their policy platforms do not consider the macroeconomic preferences of their political party as well as interest groups such as business, finance, and labor.

For monetary policy, the Fed chair may have difficulty gaining reappointment from the president if monetary policy does not take into consideration the macroeconomic preferences of the administration, voters, political parties, interest groups, and the media. One issue is that political pressure from voters and other outside influences on discretionary policy could be naïve, shortsighted, or biased. Policymakers might be swayed to adopt unsustainable policies that act against the long-term macroeconomic interests of society.

A monetary policy rule, although controversial, is one proposal for addressing the potential problem of shortsighted political influence on discretionary monetary policy. According to this concept, a mathematical rule is created to govern money supply. This fixed rule is mathematically based on macroeconomic criteria. This contrasts with the present process of discretionary judgment by the FOMC. One possible policy rule is that money supply growth equals a constant rate plus some parameter times the unemployment gap:

$$Money\ growth = constant + \beta\ (actual\ unemployment\ rate \\ - natural\ unemployment\ rate)$$

Money supply growth is equal to a constant level (of say 3 percent) if the economy is at full employment. An efficient economy occurs if actual unemployment equals the natural rate. If the economy is weak at an unemployment level greater than the natural rate, then money supply growth automatically increases based on the parameter β in the policy rule. This higher money growth leads to lower interest rates, higher macroeconomic demand, and less unemployment. If the economy is overheated at unemployment that is less than the natural rate, then money supply growth automatically decreases based on the policy rule. Consequently, interest rates rise and macroeconomic demand declines to reduce inflationary pressures.

A criticism against the concept of a monetary policy rule is that the method is too rigid in an environment of macroeconomic uncertainty. The economy might be adversely impacted by a rigid rule that is inflexible to cope with changing macroeconomic circumstances. Some uncertainty exists regarding the structure of the macroeconomy. The natural unemployment rate could be greater or less than anticipated by the policy rule. A rule that is mistaken in its assumption of natural unemployment could cause money growth to be too strong or too weak.

A policy rule that overestimates natural unemployment causes money supply growth to be too slow. The economy consequently recovers too slowly from a recession. Alternatively, the policy rule might underestimate natural unemployment. This causes money supply growth to be too rapid and creates inflationary overheating. Some uncertainty also occurs on the size of the impact of stabilization policy. A monetary policy rule that overestimates its impact causes money growth to be too weak, which leads to slow economic growth. A rule that underestimates its impact on the economy cause money growth to be too strong, which triggers rising inflation.

In other words, a policy rule that misgauges the economy creates detrimental effects. Discretionary policy, of course, is also susceptible to misjudgments by the FOMC that could harm the economy. The Fed could erroneously adopt discretionary policy that is too weak, which leads to slow economic growth. The central bank might mistakenly adopt discretionary policy that is too strong, causing higher inflation.

A discretionary monetary policy, however, has one attribute that seems advantageous over the policy rule. A discretionary policy is not locked in place in the same way that a mathematical policy rule is fixed.

A discretionary policy has more flexibility to respond to changing circumstances and misjudgments about the macroeconomic structure. The Fed, through discretionary measures, can readily adjust money supply and interest rates, based on new information, changing macroeconomic situations, or revised analyses.

A policy rule could also be revised. The process, however, may be more complex than discretionary policy. One of the main purposes of the policy rule, after all, is to make changes in policy more difficult to implement. The policy rule intentionally inhibits changes in money supply as a way to limit political interference. The process to modify a policy rule would probably require more steps than discretionary policy. Modification of the parameters in the monetary policy rule would presumably require some type of consensus or vote among the policy-rule makers, presumably the FOMC. Furthermore, if the policy rule is frequently changed, then the result is the same as discretionary policy. Shifts in discretionary policy can occur relatively fast based on the opinions of the policymakers. For these reasons, the flexibility of discretionary policy may be preferable to a rigid policy rule.

CHAPTER 10

Economic Influence on Public Sentiment and Voter Behavior

Introduction

This chapter explores the subject of economic influence on citizen opinions and voter behavior. We consider the presidential vote, Congressional House and Senate elections, the voter participation rate, macropartisanship, consumer sentiment, and the social happiness index. The chapter explains three theories of economic influence on voter behavior. They are the responsibility hypothesis, the issue hypothesis, and the salient goal hypothesis. The chapter also discusses electoral efficiency in relation to economic influence on public attitudes. In addition, we consider the political capital effect. This is the impact of the economy on presidential approval and the corresponding spillover effect on public support for the president's political and legislative agenda. Finally, we examine some important noneconomic effects on voter sentiment.

Macroeconomic Accountability and Electoral Efficiency

Voters hold the president and the in-party to the White House accountable for the health of the economy. Macroeconomic events, however, are not solely attributable to the actions of the president and the in-party. The president does not fully determine macroeconomic policies or the economic outcomes that arise from those policies.

The political interaction among the president and the Congress in association with the right and left political parties determines fiscal policy, while the central bank directly determines monetary policy. Several other factors also affect the economy, such as energy costs, commercial technology, macroeconomic policy lag and uncertainty, business cycle momentum, exogenous shocks, special interest influence on policymakers, and the frequent occurrence of partisan gridlock among the fiscal policymakers. Additionally, war, the weather, and natural disasters impact the economy.

Regardless of the various influences on the economy, voters generally hold the president and the in-party to the White House accountable for what happens. The president receives strong public approval if high economic growth occurs. This high approval rating tends to happen regardless of whether the incumbent's policies create the favorable macroeconomic outcome. The president receives low approval from the electorate if a weak economy takes place. This tends to occur regardless of whether the slow economy is attributable to the president's policy actions.

Democratic or electoral efficiency occurs if citizens elect the political candidate to the presidency whose policy agenda yields the greatest long-term economic benefit for society. Actual voter behavior, however, inevitably exhibits some amount of inefficiency. This occurs because of imperfect information and imperfect rationality among voters. Electoral inefficiency takes place if citizens elect a politician whose policies do not yield the greatest long-run economic benefit for society. This happens if voters support a president's policy that ends up making the economy worse. Citizens, for example, may be fooled into supporting a policy of macroeconomic overstimulation that creates only a temporary improvement in unemployment that comes at the cost of greater inflation in the long run.

Democratic inefficiency also arises if voters approve of the president because of a strong economy that is due to factors other than the president's policies. Suppose high economic growth takes place because of commercial technological advancements or cheap energy costs rather than the macroeconomic program of the president. Presidential approval, nevertheless, is likely to be high, as voters give credit to the president for the economic outcome. Electoral inefficiency similarly develops if the public disapproves of a president's policy that improves the economy in the long run, but with short-term adverse effects. Presidential approval, for example, is likely to decline if contractionary macroeconomic policy

causes a temporary rise in unemployment, but ultimately makes the economy better off because of a permanent decline in inflation.

Electoral inefficiency also happens if presidential approval decreases
because of a slow economy that is caused by factors other than the administration's policies. Suppose a recession transpires because of an energy
shock or a financial crisis rather than poor macroeconomic management
by the president and the in-party. Presidential approval, nevertheless, falls,
despite the weak economy being unrelated to the administration's actions.

Electoral inefficiency, in other words, occurs if the public praises or
condemns the president for macroeconomic events that the administration's policies do not create. Voters tend to judge an administration for
economic conditions that are unrelated to the president's actions. Some
ambiguity, however, exists concerning the part of economic performance
that is attributable to the president versus the portion of economic performance that is from other causes. Macroeconomic influence on voter opinions is not a perfectly efficient process. Inefficiency occurs to the degree
that voters cast votes based on economic events that transpire, without
recognizing if the in-party's policies caused the outcomes or not.

A vigilant media and farsightedness among politicians and other opinion leaders can help to promote a rationally informed economic society
and greater electoral efficiency. Some degree of democratic inefficiency,
however, seems inevitable. Some citizens cast votes based on misinforma-
tion, habit, emotion, bias, or other irrationalities. This might be reduced
but probably cannot be completely eliminated because of human nature.
Nevertheless, to the extent that voter behavior becomes more rationally
informed on the economy and other issues is the degree to which electoral
efficiency increases.

Economic and Noneconomic Effects on Presidential Elections and Presidential Approval

Presidential job approval is an estimate of the percentage of the public
that approves of the incumbent's handling of his or her job. Several organizations, such as the *Gallup Poll*, conduct regular surveys of presidential
approval and various other measures of public opinion on the incumbent.
Besides presidential approval, the most substantive public judgment of

the incumbent is presidential elections. The in-party presidential vote share is the percentage of the two-party vote in favor of the in-party candidate in a presidential election. Although not identical measurements, both presidential approval and the in-party presidential vote have parallel characteristics. Both indicators reflect public perceptions on the president's effectiveness. Accordingly, some of the explanatory variables are similar for both presidential approval and the in-party presidential vote share, while other determinants are different between the two indicators.

Economic Influence on Presidential Elections and Incumbent Popularity

The economy affects presidential job approval and presidential election outcomes in a similar manner. Three main theories have been proposed to explain economic influence on government popularity, presidential elections, and presidential job approval (Carlsen 2000). The three models are the responsibility hypothesis, the issue hypothesis, and the salient goal hypothesis.

Responsibility Hypothesis of Economic Influence on Voter Behavior

The conventional view of economic influence on voter behavior has been called the responsibility hypothesis (Carlsen 2000) or the score model (Swank 1990). This theory asserts that a strong economy causes high presidential approval and a high in-party vote share in a presidential election. A strong economy is characterized by low unemployment, high real economic growth, and low inflation. A slow economy causes low incumbent approval and a high vote share for the out-party candidate in a presidential election. The responsibility theory of voter behavior underlies the median voter model and the electoral PBC effect that are discussed in previous chapters.

The partisan PBC effect, as presented in Chapter 7, is also theoretically in line with the responsibility hypothesis of economic influence on voter actions. An implication occurs regarding the partisan PBC effect and the responsibility hypothesis. Assume the median voter model holds. The median voter theory asserts that reelection votes are highest if the in-party adopts policy that matches with the median voter's preference. Divergence of economic policy from the median voter's most preferred outcome causes presidential reelection votes for the in-party to be lower.

Suppose the president adopts a partisan economic policy instead of appealing to the median voter. The median voter's preference lies between the two partisan preferences of the left and right political parties. The conservative preference occurs to the political right of the median preference. The liberal policy preference occurs to the political left of the median voter. The in-party's probability of reelection to the White House declines if the president adopts policy based on partisan goals instead of the median voter's opinion.

Liberal presidential administrations are relatively unemployment-averse according to the partisan influence model. Expansionary policies that seek to reduce unemployment, however, can cause higher inflation if macroeconomic over-stimulus occurs. Liberal presidencies consequently risk losing the White House if high inflation arises prior to a presidential election. Citizens might choose to vote for a conservative inflation-averse president instead.

Alternatively, suppose the conservative party is in the White House. Conservative stabilization policy is more inflation-averse than the median voter's preference according to the partisan influence model. In pursuit of low inflation, unemployment may worsen because of the short-run inflation–unemployment trade-off. If this takes place prior to a presidential election, then the conservative party might lose reelection because the contractionary policy takes the economy too far to the political right of the median voter's preference. A conservative presidency is at risk to lose reelection because of the short-run effect of high unemployment from disinflationary policies. A conservative administration that focuses too much on inflation might induce voters to prefer a more liberal unemployment-averse president to be elected to the White House.

Another type of economic influence on the president may be referred to as the political capital effect. This is the impact of the economy on presidential approval and the presidency's ability to achieve its political and legislative goals. A strong economy usually causes presidential popularity to be high. This creates political capital or high public support for the administration to fulfill its political goals on issues like immigration, tax reform, health care, international trade, national defense, and the environment.

If presidential approval is high because of a strong economy, then the Congress is inclined to support the president's legislative and political program. Congressional opposition to the proposals of a popular president adversely affects the reelection prospects of legislators. Citizens might vote out of office those legislators who disagree with the plans of a popular president. A slow economy, on the other hand, causes low presidential approval. Consequently, the political capital or public support for the administration to accomplish its political and legislative agenda is likely to be weak. Congress may be inclined to challenge or oppose the proposals of an unpopular president.

Evidence on Time Consistency: The Presidential Vote versus Presidential Approval

The concept of dynamic macroeconomic consistency is compatible with the responsibility hypothesis of economic influence on voter behavior. Macroeconomic consistency occurs if the median voter's unemployment target equals the natural unemployment rate. As discussed in Chapter 2, the efficient level of unemployment is the natural unemployment rate.

If the unemployment target equals the natural rate, the median voter is rationally informed and farsighted. The median voter's preferred macroeconomic outcome is dynamically consistent because the preference is in line with what the economy can sustain. If the median voter is misinformed or shortsighted, then the median unemployment target is less than the natural rate. This preference is dynamically inconsistent because the preferred outcome is not in line with what the economy can maintain.

The research on presidential elections and presidential approval yields somewhat mixed results on whether the median voter's unemployment target is dynamically consistent or dynamically inconsistent. Some empirical findings on presidential elections imply that the median voter's macroeconomic preference is shortsighted and dynamically inconsistent (e.g., Fox 2013). This suggest citizens are willing to embrace a short-term improvement in the economy that comes at the cost of greater long-term inflation. The possibility of macroeconomic inconsistency by the median voter enables the electoral cycle effect to occur, as discussed in Chapter 6.

Some of the research in the presidential approval literature seems to imply the reverse result. These empirical findings suggest the median macroeconomic preference may be farsighted and dynamically consistent (Fox 2003, 2009; Smyth and Dua 1989). If voters are farsighted, they oppose opportunistic policies by the president to temporarily boost economic growth which comes at the cost of higher long-term inflation. If the median voter's unemployment target is dynamically consistent, then opportunistic policies cause the presidential reelection vote share for the in-party to decrease rather than increase. Voters are not fooled into supporting opportunistic policies. Instead, voters penalize presidents who attempt such strategies with lower presidential approval and lower reelection votes. Overall, the empirical results are mixed on whether the median voter's preference is dynamically consistent or inconsistent. However, if voters lack understanding on how the macroeconomy works, then the risk of dynamic inconsistency is at least present.

Clientele and Salient Goal Hypotheses of Economic Influence on Voters

The second theory of economic influence on presidential elections and presidential approval has been called the clientele hypothesis (Carlsen 2000) or the issue model or the partisan vote model (Swank 1990). This theory asserts that voter behavior emphasizes the different macroeconomic priorities of the left party and the right party.

The issue model maintains that citizens cast votes based on which of the two main parties is best suited to resolve the more important economic problem at a particular time. This theory of voting behavior is compatible with the partisan influence model that liberal administrations are relatively unemployment-averse and conservative presidencies are relatively inflation-averse. According to the issue model, citizens vote for the left party if unemployment is high compared to inflation. Voters prefer liberal presidencies if unemployment is high because of the liberal party's reputation of unemployment aversion. Citizens vote for the conservative party in presidential elections if inflation is high compared to unemployment. This occurs because of the conservative party's reputation of emphasizing low inflation in macroeconomic policy.

The issue model of voting behavior is supported by the empirical findings of Swank (1995). His analysis found that high unemployment causes public approval to increase for Democratic presidencies, while high inflation causes popularity to increase for Republican administrations.

The third model of economic influence on presidential approval and presidential elections has been called the salient goal hypothesis (Carlsen 2000). This theory of voter behavior is also compatible with the partisan PBC effect that conservative presidencies focus on reducing inflation, while liberal presidencies focus on reducing unemployment. The salient goal model asserts that voters judge presidencies by how well they attain their partisan goals. Voters approve of presidencies that succeed in their partisan economic objectives. Citizens disapprove of incumbencies that fail in their partisan priorities.

Voters weigh high unemployment more heavily against Democratic presidencies. Citizens disapprove of Democratic presidencies that fail in their liberal objective of unemployment aversion. Citizens weigh high inflation more heavily against Republican administrations. Citizens disapprove of Republican presidencies that fail in their partisan macroeconomic goal of inflation aversion.

Noneconomic Effects on Presidential Elections and Incumbent Popularity

Several noneconomic considerations weigh on voter opinions of the president. One important determinant is war. Two types of war effects impact voter attitudes. They are the soldier casualty effect and the war rally effect. The casualty effect is the adverse influence of soldier deaths on citizen sentiment of the president. The larger the number of soldier casualties, the lower the incumbent approval rating and the lower the vote share in favor of the in-party in a presidential election.

The soldier casualty effect is more adverse against presidents who are war initiators compared to presidents who are war inheritors (Fox 2013). A war initiator is a president who starts a major military conflict that ends up being long and costly in terms of military fatalities over time. A war inheritor is the subsequent president of the opposing political party who inherits a long military conflict from a war-initiator administration as the result of a presidential election. Voters penalize war-initiator presidencies with a greater casualty effect on presidential approval and reelection votes than war-inheritor presidents.

An example of the war initiator effect was G.W. Bush and the Iraq War. As soldier casualties mounted in the Iraq War, presidential approval for G.W. Bush gradually declined, especially during his second term in office. This casualty effect became a major issue that contributed to the Republican loss of the White House in the 2008 election. An example of the war inheritor effect was Barrack Obama and the Iraq War that he inherited from G.W. Bush. Iraq war casualty deaths had a much smaller negative impact on presidential approval for Obama than G.W. Bush. The war-casualty effect also had little or no adverse impact on the 2012 presidential reelection victory for Obama, since he was a war inheritor.

A further example of the war-initiator and war-inheritor effects was the impact of soldier casualties on the approval ratings of President Johnson and then President Nixon. Johnson was the war-initiator, while Nixon was the war-inheritor. Vietnam War causalities severely hurt Johnson's job approval to the degree that he chose not to run for reelection in 1968. Subsequently, Nixon from the opposing political party won the White House. Since Nixon was a war-inheritor, Vietnam war casualties had a much smaller negative impact on his popularity and he easily won his reelection in 1972, despite the Vietnam War not being over.

The war rally effect is the second type of war-related influence on voter sentiment of the incumbent. War rallies are major war-related events that create a transitory boost in presidential approval. War rallies create temporary spikes in presidential popularity connected with major military victories and other major war-related events. One type of war rally is the nationalistic support for a president at the start of a war. In the G.W. Bush presidency, three war rally effects caused transitory boosts in presidential popularity. The effects were the 9/11 terrorist attack, the start of the Iraq War, and the capture of Saddam Hussein (Fox 2009). War rallies cause presidential approval to temporarily spike upward but then gradually dissipate. In contrast, the accumulation of war casualties causes presidential approval to incrementally worsen over time.

Another political influence on the in-party presidential vote share is political party duration. This refers to the length of time (the number of consecutive 4-year presidential terms) that the in-party occupies the White House. After a political party controls the White House for two or more consecutive terms, voters increasingly prefer a change of the political party in the presidency (Fair 2009).

The party-duration effect on the in-party presidential vote share does not generally occur after just one term in office. Instead, a positive incumbency effect takes place in favor of the incumbent in presidential elections after just one term. Voters exhibit a small to moderate bias in favor of the incumbent in presidential elections after one term in office, perhaps because of familiarity with the candidate. After two or more consecutive presidential terms for the in-party, the favorable incumbent effect fades, and the negative party duration effect increasingly dominates public attitudes. Voters increasingly prefer to elect the presidential candidate from the out-party (Fair 2009).

In some instances, the adverse party duration effect can cancel out a positive economic effect on a presidential election outcome. This may have been an issue in Al Gore's presidential election defeat in 2000. Although the economy was relatively strong at the time, many voters sought a change of the political party in control of the White House. In this instance, the Democrats had occupied the Oval Office for two consecutive terms under Bill Clinton. Despite the strong economy, G.W. Bush from the opposing Republican Party won the presidency in 2000, partly because of the party-duration effect.

The party-duration effect was also probably a factor in Donald Trump's presidential victory in 2016. In that election, Obama and the Democrats had occupied the White House for two consecutive terms. Despite the recovering economy in aftermath of the Great Recession, voters chose to elect the opposing Republican Party to the Oval Office partly because of the party-duration effect.

Three additional noneconomic determinants affect presidential approval but have little or no impact on the presidential vote. They are the honeymoon effect, the scandal effect, and the opinion inertia effect. The presidential honeymoon occurs during the president's first year in office. According to the honeymoon effect, presidential popularity is relatively high immediately after an incumbent takes office after an election victory. Over a period of about one year, the initial high approval rating gradually dissipates as the election victory euphoria fades (Smyth and Dua 1989).

Presidential scandals are another noneconomic influence on presidential popularity. Some examples are the Watergate scandal on Nixon approval, the Iran–Contra scandal on Reagan approval, and the Lewinski scandal on Clinton's job approval. The Watergate and Iran–Contra scandals negatively impacted presidential approval for Nixon and Reagan. The Lewinski scandal, however, had a positive impact on Clinton's popularity. In this case, many voters viewed the impeachment against Clinton as excessive, and subsequently the Senate acquitted Clinton of the House impeachment. After the acquittal, Clinton's popularity spiked upward.

The opinion inertia effect is a third noneconomic influence on incumbent popularity. Because of opinion persistence or inertia among voters, presidential approval tends to change gradually in response to changes in the economy. A sustained improvement in the economy has a small initial impact on presidential approval. This small effect increases in magnitude over the subsequent months if the strong economy persists.

Economic Influence on Congressional Elections

The economy also influences Congressional House election results. The Congressional House vote share for the in-party is the percentage of the two-party vote in favor of in-party candidates in House of Representatives elections. Two types of Congressional House elections occur, which are on-term elections and midterm elections. The on-term House vote refers to Congressional elections that take place in the same years as the presidential vote. The 2016 Congressional election was an on-term vote year because a presidential election took place. The midterm vote refers to Congressional House elections that occur between presidential elections. The 2018 Congressional vote was a midterm election because a presidential election did not take place that year.

The economy influences Congressional House election outcomes for both on-term and midterm elections. The impact of the economy, however, is different for on-term elections versus midterm elections. Economic influence on on-term House elections occurs indirectly through the presidential coattail effect. Economic influence on midterm House elections takes place indirectly through the presidential approval effect.

The on-term House vote share for in-party political candidates is directly correlated with the in-party presidential vote share. This is the presidential coattail effect. If the in-party wins a presidential election because of a strong economy or other factors, then the in-party Congressional House vote share likewise tends to increase. The more the votes for the presidential candidate of the incumbent party, the greater the in-party House vote share. If a low vote share occurs for the presidential candidate of the in-party because of a weak economy or other factors, then the in-party Congressional House vote share similarly tends to decline. The House vote share, in other words, increases for the political party that wins the presidential election. If a Democrat wins the White House, then Democrats are likely to gain votes and seats in the House of Representatives. If a Republican wins the presidency, then Republicans likely gain votes and seats in the House.

In midterm elections, the economy indirectly impacts the in-party House vote share through the presidential approval effect. The stronger is the economy, the greater is presidential approval, and the larger the vote share for in-party candidates in midterm House elections. The weaker is the economy, the lower is presidential approval, and the lower is the in-party midterm House vote share. If presidential approval for a Republican president is high because of a strong economy or other factors, then Republicans may gain seats in the House in a midterm election. If presidential approval for a Republican president is low because of a weak economy or other factors, then Democrats may gain seats in the House in a midterm election.

A noneconomic determinant on midterm House elections is the balancing effect. The midterm balancing effect partially offsets or counteracts the on-term presidential coattail. Through the coattail effect, the House vote share in on-term elections increases for the political party that wins the White House. For midterm elections, the in-party tends to lose House votes and seats as citizens reduce their support for the in-party. Citizens tend to vote for the out-party in midterm elections. Perhaps this occurs because some in-party campaign promises from the on-term election tend to go unfulfilled by the time of the subsequent midterm election. The public tends to vote for the out-party in midterm House elections through the balancing effect, whereas in on-term elections citizens tend to vote for House candidates who belong to the political party that wins the Oval Office through the presidential coattail effect.

The economy affects Senate election outcomes similar to the way the economy influences House elections. Campbell and Sumners (1990) found that the economy indirectly affects the in-party Senate vote share in on-term elections through the presidential coattail. If the in-party wins the White House because of a strong economy or other factors, then the in-party Senate vote share likewise increases. For midterm elections, Abramowitz and Segal (1992) found that the economy indirectly affects Senate election outcomes through the presidential popularity effect. If the economy causes presidential approval to rise prior to the midterm vote, then the in-party's share of Senate seats may go up in midterm elections.

Their analysis also found a balancing effect in midterm Senate elections analogous to the effect on House elections. Other things held equal, the in-party often suffers seat losses in both the Senate and the House during midterm elections. Voters tend to increase support for the out-party in midterm elections. This balancing effect in favor of out-party Congressional candidates in midterm elections partially or wholly negates the coattail effect in favor of in-party Congressional candidates in on-term elections.

Other Measures of Public Sentiment Relating to the Economy

Besides economic influence on election outcomes, macroeconomic events affect other indicators of citizen attitudes. Consumer sentiment, for example, is a measure of public perceptions and expectations on the health of the economy. The Survey of Consumer Sentiment by the University of Michigan is the most well-known measurement. The index of consumer sentiment is based on survey responses from households. Consumer expectations about the economy are optimistic if consumer sentiment is high. Consumer expectations about the economy are pessimistic if the consumer sentiment index is low. The state of the economy affects consumer sentiment, especially unemployment and inflation.

Consumer confidence tends to be high or optimistic if unemployment and inflation are low. Consumer confidence among households becomes pessimistic if inflation and unemployment are high.

Some other measures of public sentiment that are affected by the economy are macropartisanship, voter turnout or the voter participation rate, and societal happiness. Macropartisanship is a political indicator of the distribution of aggregate voter partisanship across the population. This partisanship indicator estimates the percentage of citizens who identify with each of the two major political parties. The percentage of voters who identify with the in-party tends to rise if the economy is strong. The percentage of the public who identify with the in-party tends to decline if economic performance is low. If, for example, the president is a Democrat and economic growth is high, then the percentage of voters who identify with the Democratic Party will probably rise (MacKuen, Erikson, and Stimson 1989).

Voter turnout or the voter participation rate is the percentage of the adult populace who decide to vote in presidential (and other) elections. An economic determinant that has been found to influence voter turnout in presidential elections is unemployment. The level of voter turnout in presidential elections tends to be low if unemployment is low. Low unemployment may cause voters to feel satisfied with their economic situation. Consequently, they may be less inclined to vote because of economic contentment. The voter participation rate tends to be high if unemployment is high. A high unemployment rate causes political and economic dissatisfaction among voters. Consequently, the public has a greater urgency to vote to motivate politicians to remedy the economic distress.

The social happiness index is an additional measure of public opinion that is affected by the economy. The social happiness indicator, based on survey responses, provides an estimate of the level of public well-being. The higher the happiness index, the greater the attitude of well-being among the population. A strong economy—such as low unemployment, low inflation, and high income growth—tends to cause the happiness index to rise. A weak economy causes the social happiness index to decrease (Frey and Stutzer 2002).

CHAPTER 11

Trade Policies and International Political Perspectives

Introduction

This chapter examines two international topics with political macroeconomic ramifications. The first subject is the political economy of free trade versus trade protectionism. This subject partially overlaps with the second topic. The second topic is a comparison of the three ideological perspectives of economic liberalism, neomercantilism, and economic structuralism. These three international perspectives provide insights on the political and economic implications of international trade policy and globalism.

Relation between Net Exports, GDP, Unemployment, and the Exchange Rate

A commonly used measure of international trade is net exports or the trade balance. Net exports is equal to exports minus imports (NX = X – M). Exports are domestically produced goods that are transported and sold to buyers in foreign nations. Imports are foreign-produced goods that are transported and sold to buyers in the receiving country. A trade surplus occurs if exports exceed imports. A trade deficit occurs if imports are greater than exports.

One of the four main components of GDP is net exports. GDP and net exports are mathematically related based on the GDP accounting identity. GDP = C + I + G + NX, where C is consumption, I is gross investment, and G is government spending. From an accounting point of view, a trade surplus causes GDP to increase by the amount of the surplus. A trade deficit causes GDP to decline by the amount of the deficit. Suppose GDP is initially equal to $20 trillion with a trade balance of zero (X = M or NX = 0). Now, assume a trade deficit of $0.5 trillion ($500 billion) occurs. GDP declines from $20 trillion to $19.5 trillion. Suppose a trade surplus of $0.5 trillion occurs. GDP rises from $20 trillion to $20.5 trillion.

Historically, the United States ran trade surpluses during most years after WWII until the early 1970s. This occurred partly because the United States emerged as the dominant economic power following the World War II. The economic infrastructure of the United States including export industries was unharmed from the devastation of WWII that occurred overseas. Most of the military conflicts of WWII took place in Europe, Asia, and North Africa.

After WWII, many of the countries in Europe, Asia, and elsewhere required several years to rebuild their war-torn economies. By the 1970s, however, they had largely reestablished their economies. The United States consequently began experiencing trade deficits as the economies of Europe and Japan became more trade competitive. Since the 1970s, the U.S. trade deficit has gradually worsened as the global economy has become even more economically competitive.

Figure 11.1 shows the pattern of U.S. net exports as a percentage of GDP in the post-WWII era. The solid line in the graph is net exports as a percentage of GDP. The dashed line is the unemployment rate. The shaded areas denote time periods of economic recession.

The accounting relation between net exports and GDP may be somewhat misleading in understanding the interconnection between the trade deficit and GDP. A smaller trade deficit causes higher GDP based on the accounting measurement. This effect is important but often not the dominant influence. The impact of GDP on the trade deficit is frequently greater than the impact of the trade deficit on GDP.

Higher GDP is often associated with a larger trade deficit, not a smaller trade deficit as the accounting suggests. National income is closely

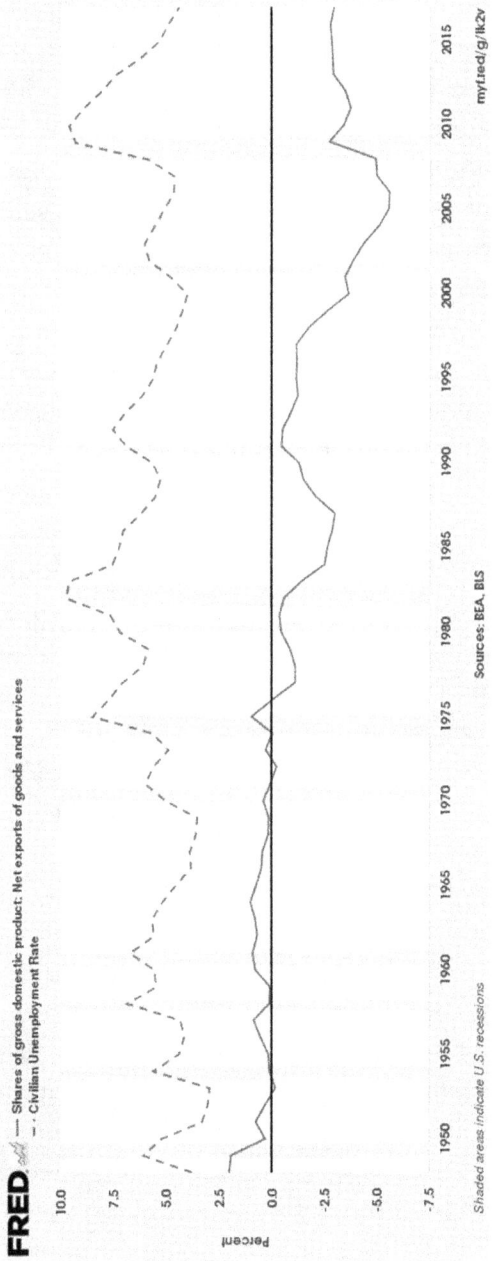

Figure 11.1 Relation between net exports and unemployment

linked to GDP. National income equals GDP minus depreciation of capital in the economy. Higher national income generally occurs alongside higher GDP. Higher national income enables households and businesses to increase their purchases. This is the consumption function effect.

Higher income enables greater spending. A portion of higher spending is on more imports. This reduces or worsens net exports. Consequently, the trade deficit often becomes worse during periods of high economic growth and declining unemployment. On the other hand, the trade deficit frequently improves or becomes smaller during periods of declining GDP, recession, and rising unemployment.

Lower GDP and rising unemployment are associated with lower national income. Lower income leads to lower business and consumer spending. This includes less spending on imports. As imports decrease, the trade deficit improves or becomes smaller.

Figure 11.1 shows these results. The trade deficit as a percentage of GDP improved during many (but not all) of the economic recessions. The trade deficit, for example, was large at about 5.5 percent of GDP in 2005 when the U.S. economy was strong prior to the Great Recession of 2007–2009. At the same time, unemployment was low at about 5 percent in 2005 prior to the Great Recession.

Unemployment worsened during the Great Recession to around 10 percent. The trade deficit consequently became smaller at around 2.5 percent of GDP during this period. The trade deficit improved during the Great Recession because income fell alongside higher unemployment. Fewer jobs led to less income and less spending, including less spending on imports. As imports fell, the trade deficit became smaller. The smaller trade deficit occurred alongside lower GDP and worsening unemployment during the Great Recession.

Besides national income and GDP, another major factor that affects the trade deficit is the exchange rate. The exchange rate affects the prices of traded goods and the amounts of traded goods.

An increase in the exchange rate is the same thing as a currency appreciation or a stronger currency. An appreciation of the currency means the domestic currency can buy more units of a foreign currency. A stronger currency causes import prices to fall and export prices to rise. Based on the law of demand, imports increase as import prices go down. Additionally, exports decline as export prices go up. The trade deficit worsens when the currency appreciates.

A decrease in the exchange rate denotes a currency devaluation or a weaker currency. A decrease in the value of the currency means the domestic currency can buy less units of a foreign currency. A weaker currency causes import prices to become more expensive while export prices become cheaper. Based on the law of demand, imports fall as import prices go up. Additionally, exports rise as export prices fall. The trade deficit tends to become smaller because of a stronger currency.

In summary, two main determinants that affect the trade deficit are national income or GDP and exchange rates. A stronger dollar and higher economic growth tend to make the trade deficit worse. A weaker dollar and lower economic growth, especially a recession, tend to make the trade deficit smaller.

Comparative Advantage, Free Trade, and Economic Liberalism

According to the theory of comparative advantage, the most efficient approach to international trade is through competitive market forces. Comparative advantage asserts that international trade should be relatively unimpeded by government intervention such as import tariffs and quotas. An import tariff is a tax on imports, while an import quota is a quantity restriction on imports. The theory of comparative advantage recommends free trade policy. Free trade occurs through competitive market forces unhindered by government intervention. With free trade, businesses and households are free to buy and sell exports and imports through supply and demand forces.

The theory of comparative advantage maintains that countries should specialize in producing and exporting economic goods that they can supply relatively cheaper than other nations. Countries should import products that other nations can provide relatively cheaper. According to comparative advantage, free trade through competitive market forces generally creates win-win economic outcomes among nations. Free trade enables countries to increase consumption of products beyond what would occur without trade. Free trade enables more exports and more imports to occur across nations, which generates greater spending and higher world economic growth.

The economic theory of comparative advantage should not be confused with the similar-sounding strategic business management concept of competitive advantage. The idea of competitive advantage was developed by Michael Porter in his book entitled *Competitive Advantage of Nations* (1985). The concept of competitive advantage refers to the strategies and abilities of businesses and industries to compete with domestic and international business rivals. Competitive advantage strategies emphasize providing customers with increased product value through approaches such as low production costs and low prices, product differentiation, and target markets.

The trade theory of comparative advantage, on the other hand, is associated with the ideological perspective of economic liberalism. The root word of *liberalism* is *liberty*. The perspective of economic liberalism considers the concepts of *economic liberty* and *economic freedom* as basically synonymous with the idea of competitive market forces. Economic liberalism emphasizes the positive outcomes of economic freedom or competitive market forces such as innovation, productivity, business competition, and efficiency.

Economic liberalism emphasizes that through free trade consumers benefit from lower product prices, increased consumption of goods, as well as increased variety and quality of products. These beneficial results are called the consumption gains from free trade. Even with a trade deficit, the economic benefits to consumers generally outweigh the potential negative effects on jobs and businesses in import-competing industries, according to economic liberalism.

Trade Protectionism and Neomercantilism

Protectionism is government intervention in international market forces to boost trade outcomes based on national economic interests. This contrasts with comparative advantage and free trade that emphasizes private economic interests among buyers and sellers through unimpeded supply and demand forces. Protectionist policies seek to reduce imports or increase exports, thereby raising net exports. An increase in net exports is associated with either a larger trade surplus or a smaller trade deficit. In either case, higher net exports cause higher GDP.

Trade protectionism seeks to boost the national economy through higher net exports, which causes higher GDP and by extension lower unemployment. The political left is more likely to embrace trade protectionism than the political right. This is because the political left is more inclined toward government intervention in the economy to remedy perceptions of market failure.

Trade barriers such as import tariffs and quotas are used to reduce imports and protect import-competing industries. Free trade can harm business performance and employment in import-competing industries. For example, manufacturing industries in the United States and other developed countries face international trade competition from lesser-developed countries such as China, India, and Mexico. These countries have a comparative advantage in basic manufacturing because of lower wages, lower production costs, and lower product prices. Trade protectionism reduces the inflow of imports that are less expensive than domestically produced goods. From a comparative advantage and economic liberalism perspective, an adverse effect of trade protectionism such as import quotas and tariffs is economic harm to consumers. Tariffs and quotas typically cause higher import prices for consumers.

Political Pressures on Trade Policy

Public sentiment, special interests, the media, opinion leaders, and political parties exert pressure on elected officials to influence international trade policies. Political pressure for trade protectionism occurs in response to economic harm to import-competing industries. This includes lost jobs and weak business performance in import-competing industries. In contrast, political pressure in support of free trade occurs in response to economic gains such as jobs and business performance in export industries, as well as the economic benefits of imports to consumers.

Trade sanctions are another type of government intervention in international trade based on political criteria rather than economic considerations. Trade sanctions are used as an economic penalty against a country for political actions considered harmful or hostile. Trade sanctions reduce or eliminate trade with a foreign country through trade barriers such as tariffs and quotas. In a complete trade embargo, all exports and imports with a foreign country are blocked. Trade sanctions apply economic pressure on a foreign nation to induce the foreign government to alter its policies.

Trade sanctions have been used against countries for acts relating to international terrorism, human rights violations including crimes against humanity and genocide, wars, and illegally developing weapons of mass destruction (WMD). Trade sanctions are less destructive than military action against a foreign nation. Sanctions, however, often have a limited impact on causing a foreign state to modify or change its policies and actions.

Trade sanctions can harm consumers in the affected country. Sanctions may limit important consumer imports such as food and medicine. Sanctions also hurt business activity and employment in industries in the foreign country that rely on trade. The elites in a country may be able to maintain a wealthy lifestyle while low-income households and small businesses are economically hurt by trade sanctions.

For example, a dictator in a rogue state may refuse to alter policies, such as development of WMD. Consequently, trade sanctions may be imposed. This could end up harming those who are poor in the country rather than the dictator. The trade sanctions could backfire. Imports of food and medicine could be cut because of the sanctions. The economic hardship caused by trade sanctions could create public animosity against the government issuing the sanctions.

Trade sanctions are often effective in economically penalizing a country. The affected country, however, may be able to partially negate the negative impact of sanctions by increasing trade with other nations. Consequently, multiple countries may need to simultaneously adopt trade sanctions for the policy to work.

Sanctions often harm those who are economically vulnerable while frequently being ineffective in causing a regime to modify its actions. To increase effectiveness, a punitive trade sanction could be combined with a positive offer. For example, foreign aid could be offered in exchange for compliance with the terms of the country issuing the trade sanction. A carrot-and-stick approach may have greater success than trade sanctions alone.

Mercantilism and Neomercantilism

Mercantilism was a nationalistic trade approach adopted by some European countries such as England and France from the 16th to the 19th centuries during the gold standard era. Mercantilist policies were adopted to increase exports, reduce imports, and, if possible, attain trade surpluses. A primary goal of mercantilism was gold and silver accumulation through exportation of goods. Countries were typically required to pay gold and silver to their trade partners to cover a trade deficit.

In the mercantilist system, international trade affected the national accumulation of precious metals, the money supply, and product prices through the price–specie flow mechanism. A country with a trade surplus increased its accumulation of gold and silver. The trade-surplus country was paid gold and silver in exchange for its exports to its trade partners. This caused the nation's money supply to rise because of the gold standard. The amount of money in circulation was tied to the amount of gold held by the government. Higher money supply typically caused higher inflation. Exports consequently became more expensive because of inflation. This ultimately led to less exports and a declining trade surplus.

In contrast, a country with a trade deficit experienced declining stockpiles of gold and silver. The trade-deficit country paid gold and silver in exchange for imports received from its trade partners. This caused the country's money supply to decline and price deflation. Exports therefore became cheaper. This led to more exports and a shrinking trade deficit.

Trade mercantilism during the gold standard era evolved into modern neomercantilism of the 20th and 21st centuries in the post-gold standard era. Neomercantilism means new mercantilism. Trade barriers were used to increase net exports to acquire gold and silver in the mercantilist period. In modern neomercantilism, protectionist trade barriers are used to increase net exports, GDP, national income, employment, and international reserves (foreign currencies) in the banking system. Some examples of neomercantilist or protectionist policies besides import quotas and tariffs include production subsidies, export subsidies, trade dumping, and exchange rate devaluation.

Neomercantilist trade policies seek to boost the economy through increasing exports or reducing imports. An export-led growth strategy consists of neomercantilist policies designed to raise exports such as export subsidies and trade dumping. Export subsidies consist of government financial assistance to businesses to promote exports. Some examples of export subsidies are monetary grants, special tax concessions, or low-interest loans.

An import-substitution strategy is trade protectionism designed to reduce imports. A production subsidy is an example of an import-substitution policy. A production subsidy is government financial assistance to businesses to increase their production at lower after-subsidy costs and prices. This enables business firms to be more price-competitive against imports. Production subsidies are typically in the form of financial grants, tax breaks, and low-interest loans.

Exchange rate manipulation is another kind of protectionist or neomercantilist policy to influence international trade. An exchange rate devaluation affects the prices of traded goods so that exports increase while imports decrease, thereby causing net exports to rise. Imports become more expensive and exports become cheaper through a currency devaluation. Based on the law of demand, imports decline as import prices rise, while exports increase as export prices go down. Net exports consequently increase from a protectionist currency devaluation.

Two types of exchange rate regimes may occur. They are fixed or pegged exchange rates and flexible or floating exchange rates. The government directly determines the level for a fixed exchange rate. A protectionist currency devaluation occurs by government action in a fixed exchange rate regime. The government sets the exchange rate at a weaker level, which improves net exports through the effect on the prices of exports and imports.

In contrast, market forces determine the level of a flexible exchange rate. Attaining the intended result of a protectionist currency depreciation is more difficult in a flexible exchange rate regime than for a fixed exchange rate. The government or central bank must sell a large amount of domestic currency in the foreign exchange market to cause a noticeable depreciation of a flexible exchange rate. If the currency is a major hard currency with substantial international usage, such as the U.S. dollar, then the government action of selling dollars in the foreign exchange market would likely have a minimal impact. A vast amount of U.S. dollars already exists in the foreign exchange market throughout the world. A government attempt to flood the foreign exchange market with more dollars would probably have a small effect on the total supply of dollars and therefore a small depreciating effect on the currency.

Trade neomercantilism may be offensive or defensive in nature. Offensive neomercantilism may be referred to as beggar-thy-neighbor policies, unfair trade, or exporting unemployment. Unfair trade or offensive neomercantilism occurs if exports and imports violate international laws and norms. Offensive neomercantilism uses trade barriers to aggressively boost net exports, jobs, and GDP. This comes at an economic cost to the trade partner. The trade partner experiences reduced net exports, GDP, and employment. This is sometimes called *exporting unemployment.* An increase in net exports for one country causes a decline in net exports for the trade partner. The neomercantilist perspective suggests that international trade is often a zero-sum game with win-lose results. Countries with trade surpluses gain economically, while countries with trade deficits are harmed economically.

Defensive neomercantilism is the punitive use of trade barriers against unfair trade. Defensive neomercantilism is protectionist trade retaliation against unfair trade practices. The goal of defensive neomercantilism is to induce an unfair trade partner to discontinue aggressive protectionism and adopt a more conciliatory or mutually beneficial trade policy. Defensive neomercantilism attempts to induce an unfair trade partner through punitive protectionism to adopt a fairer trade policy.

The danger of protectionist retaliation against unfair trade is that international tensions could worsen between the countries. The trade partner could retaliate further with additional trade barriers. A trade war could arise. A trade war is the escalation of trade protectionism between nations that reduces the volume of trade and economically harms both trade partners. A trade war creates a negative-sum or lose-lose economic outcome. The risk of neomercantilist policies, whether offensive or defensive, is that a trade war occurs. Diminished trade from escalating trade barriers consequently takes place, and slower economic growth occurs for both trade partners.

A neomercantilist reaction against globalism arose in the United Kingdom and the United States in 2016. This anti-globalism sentiment could be interpreted as a populist reaction to the debt crises and economic hardship caused by the Great Recession a few years earlier. Anti-globalism appeared to intensify during and following the Great Recession. In June of 2016, the majority of U.K. citizens voted in favor of the Brexit referendum to withdraw from the European Union. Then, in November of 2016, Donald Trump was elected as U.S. president. Subsequently, American foreign policy shifted to a more protectionist stance on trade and other international issues such as immigration, environmental treaties, and NATO.

The following year, in 2017, France elected Emmanuel Macron as president. His political rival in that election was Marine Le Pen. An important element of Le Pen's campaign was for France to withdraw from the European Union. The political stability of the European Union could have been jeopardized if Le Pen had won the presidential election and France had left the European Union. Instead, Macron was elected by a wide margin. France consequently remained in the European Union. An important ongoing issue, however, is whether the neomercantilist pressures in the United States and parts of Western Europe will persist or subside over time.

Economic Structuralism

In addition to economic liberalism and neomercantilism, economic structuralism is a third perspective on international trade and globalism. Economic structuralism emphasizes the harmful effects that may arise from global capitalism. According to structuralism, a major structural issue of the market system is the adverse results that may occur from the business profit incentive. If unconstrained by effective business laws and regulations, the profit drive can lead to harmful exploitation of economic resources, workers, consumers, and the environment.

Economic structuralism focuses on potential inherent problems of capitalism such as labor exploitation, consumer exploitation, environmental damage from globalism, and disparities in income and wealth within and among countries. The market system simultaneously creates wealth and poverty among and within nations according to structuralism.

Developed countries and multinational corporations tend to economically benefit from international trade and globalism. Developing countries, in contrast, may become worse off or may not economically gain from globalism to the extent of developed countries. The economic gap between rich and poor states could persist or become worse. Rich countries maintain structural advantages such as more economic resources, greater productivity of resources, a more developed economic infrastructure, a stronger educational system, more income and wealth, military and commercial technological superiority, and harder currencies. These advantages allow developed nations to maintain international economic, political, and military dominance. Poorer countries face structural obstacles to economic advancement. Poor countries often find it difficult to economically compete with richer states.

Modern World Systems View and Dependency Theory

Modern economic structuralism may be further explained in terms of modern world systems theory and dependency theory. Countries may be grouped into one of three politico-economic classifications according to world systems theory. They are the industrial core, the agricultural periphery, and the economic semi-periphery. The industrial core consists mainly of developed countries. The agricultural periphery refers to many of the developing countries. The semi-periphery is composed of newly industrialized nations.

The industrial core is made up of nations and geographic regions that have a relatively high degree of economic development. This includes the United States., Canada, Western Europe, Japan, Australia, New Zealand, and Israel. The industrial core of developed nations largely determines the political, military, economic, and legal frameworks and characteristics of the global political-economic system. Countries with stronger economic and military power have greater influence on the structure of the global order. Richer countries mainly determine the rules and mechanisms of the international system, which may adversely impact the periphery and semi-periphery.

The agricultural periphery consists of economically underdeveloped nations. Geographic regions in the agricultural periphery include Central

America, much of South America, most of Africa, parts of Central and Eastern Europe, and Southeast Asia. The dominant industries of underdeveloped nations in the periphery are agriculture and natural resource extraction.

A key dynamic of the world systems theory is that industrial core exploits resources in the agricultural periphery. Through international commerce, MNCs from richer states obtain economic resources and commodities, such as raw materials, labor, and food from poor states at relatively low prices. MNCs use the commodities and resources obtained from lesser-developed countries to produce higher value-added goods at higher prices. This generates greater profitability for MNCs and higher GDP among richer nation-states.

The semi-periphery consists of nations with a level of economic development between the industrial core and the agricultural periphery. Countries in the semi-periphery exhibit some industrialization, especially in labor-intensive semiskilled manufacturing. Some examples of countries in the semi-periphery are Mexico, Argentina, Brazil, China, India, and South Korea. Countries in the semi-periphery have developed economically beyond the agricultural periphery. Countries in the semi-periphery, however, face structural difficulty advancing economically into the industrial core because of various obstacles in the global capitalist system such as gaps in technology, wealth, education, innovation, energy, and natural resources.

Structural obstacles inhibit upward economic mobility of poorer nation-states partly because of the technological advantages of the industrial core. These advantages initially arose because of the industrial revolution. The industrial revolution began in Great Britain in the late 18th century. Over the subsequent decades, the industrial revolution spread to other nations in Europe, such as Belgium, Germany, and France, as well as to North America and Japan.

According to world systems theory, this group of countries developed into the industrial core. They gained a commercial technological advantage in manufacturing at the time of the industrial revolution. The industrial core achieved a technological head start because they were the first countries to take advantage of manufacturing technology. The industrial core has been able to maintain a commercial and military technological advantage since the time of the industrial revolution. The technological advantages of the industrial core have been sustained through continual innovation and development of new commercial and military advancements. Most technological breakthroughs take place in the industrial core and are later transferred to the periphery and semi-periphery through international business activity.

Dependency theory is a further extension of modern economic structuralism. Lesser-developed countries in the agricultural periphery are vulnerable to the policies and actions of richer nations. The lopsided international power structure adversely impacts poorer countries. The agricultural periphery and the semi-periphery may be coerced to conform with the political and economic agenda of the industrial core.

Rich states possess the economic and military power to reward or punish poorer countries based on whether poor states support or oppose the agenda of rich states. If poor countries support the policies of the industrial core, they may be rewarded with increased foreign aid, favorable trade relations, international investment, technology transfer, and military protection. These actions lead to increased jobs and economic growth among poorer states. In contrast, if poorer countries resist the economic and political agenda of the industrial core, then poor nations could be penalized with reduced trade and investment, declining foreign aid, reduced technology transfer, and reduced military protection. These policies adversely affect the jobs, the economic growth, and the political stability of poorer states.

Summary

The political economy of free trade versus protectionism examines the various political and economic effects of the two opposing policy approaches. The concept of free trade emphasizes the beneficial results of competitive market forces on international trade, especially for consumers. Comparative advantage theory prescribes free trade with minimal government intervention. Comparative advantage theory asserts that countries should specialize in producing and exporting goods in which they are relatively more productive. Nations should import goods from other countries in which the latter are relatively more productive.

Comparative advantage and free trade are aspects of the economic liberalism perspective. Economic liberalism maintains that free trade through competitive international market forces generally creates win-win economic outcomes among nations. In general, free trade is mutually beneficial across countries. The ideal approach to global economic growth for both rich and poor countries alike is through free trade. The political right tends to be a stronger advocate than the political left for free trade. The political right tends to have greater confidence in market forces.

The neomercantilist perspective asserts that trade protectionism is often necessary to protect national economic interest. Neomercantilism sees international economic relations, including trade, as often generating win-lose economic outcomes. Countries with trade surpluses gain, while countries with trade deficits are harmed. Trade barriers are often needed to increase net exports, jobs, and GDP. The political left is generally more likely than the political right to embrace trade protectionism. The political left is more inclined to support government intervention in the economy, including trade barriers, because of perceptions of market failure.

Economic structuralism views international trade and global capitalism as often detrimental to poor countries while enriching developed countries. Globalism simultaneously creates prosperity and poverty. In a worse-case scenario, rich countries become wealthier while the poor states remain impoverished. More realistically, rich countries become wealthier while many poor countries also become richer but often not enough to reduce income disparities between rich and poor nations. Economic structuralism views globalism as often generating win-lose outcomes. Developed countries attain greater economic growth than many poor states because of structural problems inherent in the capitalist system.

To alleviate the wealth and income gaps among rich and poor states, economic structuralism recommends that richer countries should economically assist poor countries in various ways such as greater foreign aid to poor countries, increased exports from poor countries to rich countries, greater technological transfer to poor states, and greater foreign direct investment in lesser-developed nations.

CHAPTER 12

Conclusion

The political macroeconomy refers to concepts, issues, and evidence on the interrelation between the economy and various political influences upon fiscal and monetary policies. Several linkages occur among macroeconomic politics, macroeconomic policies, macroeconomic policymakers, and macroeconomic events. Some important political influences on fiscal and monetary policies are partisan economic goals, presidential and Congressional reelection ambition, the president's influence on the Fed, voter behavior, interest groups, and the media. Political influence on macroeconomic policies involves the interactions among the three policymakers, which are the president, Congress, and the central bank, along with the influence of the left and right political parties.

Fiscal and monetary policies affect the economy and the pattern of the business cycle. The state of the economy impacts partisan economic priorities, presidential approval and other measures of citizen sentiment, including voter behavior and the reelection prospects of the president and members of Congress. The condition of the economy also affects political and societal stability. Prosperity and perceptions of economic fairness promote greater societal well-being. Poverty and perceptions of economic inequity breed political dissatisfaction and discord among the economic classes.

An economic ideological divide occurs between the political right and the political left on the role of government versus market forces in the economy. The ideology of the political right tends to embrace the classical economic perspective that emphasizes the advantages of competitive market forces. The ideology of the political left generally supports the Keynesian outlook of government intervention to stimulate the economy during periods of slowdown because of perceived shortcomings of market forces.

A major theme of the political macroeconomy is the conflicting economic viewpoints of the political right and the political left on fiscal and monetary policies. Conservative sentiment advocates a small governmental role in the economy. This occurs through low government spending with a strong emphasis on national defense and lesser emphasis on social programs. The political right generally recommends low taxes across all economic classes. The political right and the classical macroeconomic outlook advise minimal government regulations on business.

The political left recommends a more active governmental role in the economy. The political left advises relatively high government spending with a strong emphasis on social programs and less focus on military spending. The political left often recommends higher taxes on wealthy individuals and corporations. The liberal view advocates for increased regulations on business to protect consumers, workers, and the environment.

Active fiscal and monetary policies are necessary according to Keynesianism and the political left. This is because the economy does not always automatically adjust to cure unemployment through market forces in a timely and effective manner. Interventionist stabilization policies are necessary because economic rigidities and inefficiencies inhibit the self-correcting mechanism of market forces from reaching full employment.

The interrelation among the main macroeconomic indicators lays the foundation for examining political influences on macroeconomic policy. Three important economic indicators are Real GDP or Real GDP growth, unemployment, and inflation. These measurements affect household economic well-being, consumer sentiment, business activity, voter behavior, presidential approval, and the reelection prospects for the in-party.

Interest rates are another major economic indicator. Interest rates affect the economy through the impact on debt-financed household and business spending. International trade is also important and related to Real GDP and unemployment. The trade deficit and GDP simultaneously influence each other. An increase in imports worsens the trade deficit and causes GDP to decline. This occurs because the trade deficit is an accounting component of GDP. As GDP declines because of a trade deficit, unemployment worsens in import-competing industries. On the other hand, lower GDP and rising unemployment tend to improve the trade deficit. This occurs because less income is available for spending on imports when GDP is low.

Finally, the up-and-down pattern of the business cycle is a significant economic measurement. The expansion and contraction phases of the business cycle identify the fluctuating gap between the actual economy and an efficient economy. An efficient economy occurs at the natural unemployment rate and potential Real GDP.

The expectational Phillips curve provides a framework for understanding the short-run inflation–unemployment trade-off and the dynamics of the business cycle. In addition, Okun's law depicts the inverse correlation between RGDP growth and the change in unemployment. The expectational Phillips curve model combined with Okun's law provides an approach for examining the association among inflation, unemployment, and economic growth. The behavior of these three economic variables is important because of the impact on citizen sentiment, voter decisions, partisan priorities, and policymaker actions.

Fiscal and monetary policies affect inflation, unemployment, Real GDP, and economic growth in the short run and in the long run. The effects of stabilization policies on the economy can be analyzed using the expectational Phillips curve and Okun's law. Expansionary fiscal and monetary policies seek to expand economic growth and reduce unemployment with the possible negative side effect of rising inflation. Contractionary fiscal and monetary policies seek to reduce inflation with the possible negative side effects of slower real economic growth and rising unemployment.

Fiscal policy occurs through the political compromise between the president and Congress and involves the economic priorities of the two main political parties. Fiscal policy is the effect of taxes and government expenditures on the economy. The goal of expansionary fiscal policy is to reduce unemployment and consists of lower taxes and higher government spending. The objective of contractionary fiscal policy is to reduce inflation and consists of higher taxes or lower government spending.

Monetary policy is controlled by the Federal Open Market Committee of the Federal Reserve, with the Fed Chair playing the dominant role in leading the committee. Monetary policy is the influence of money supply and interest rates on the economy. The goal of expansionary monetary policy is to reduce unemployment and consists of higher money supply growth and lower interest rates. The purpose of contractionary monetary policy is to reduce inflation and consists of lower money supply growth and higher interest rates.

Rational voter theory maintains that the influence of the economy on public attitudes and voter behavior occurs through a rational opinion-making process. Each citizen votes for the political candidate who embraces policies that align with that voter's preferred outcome. The median voter model is based on rational voter theory. The median voter model predicts that politicians and political parties take actions that converge to the median voter's preference. This convergence arises as each of the two opposing parties compete by embracing policies that appeal more to the political center. Electoral pressures cause presidents to administer policies that align with the median voter's sentiment, especially before elections. The goal of this political strategy is to attain high presidential approval and improve reelection prospects for the in-party.

One implication of the median voter model is the electoral cycle. This effect involves the concept of macroeconomic inconsistency versus macroeconomic consistency. If the median voter is shortsighted or naïve about the economy, then the median preference is dynamically inconsistent. The electorate, in this case, may be fooled into supporting a transitory economic boom that temporarily reduces unemployment before a presidential election but with greater inflation after the election. According to the electoral effect, the incumbent opportunistically manipulates the economy through stimulative fiscal and monetary policies to create a preelection economic expansion to boost the presidential vote for the in-party.

However, if the median citizen is informed and farsighted, then the macroeconomic preference is dynamically consistent. The electorate disapproves of opportunistic policies in this case. Voters are aware of the negative inflationary side effect of manipulative policy. An attempt by the incumbent to engineer the economy for temporary gain backfires, and less votes occur for the in-party in a presidential election.

The research is mixed on whether the median voter's preference is consistent or inconsistent. Some research on presidential approval suggests that the median voter's macroeconomic preference may be dynamically consistent. But other research on the presidential vote suggests that the median preference may be inconsistent.

Besides the electoral cycle, the other main PBC effect is the partisan cycle. The partisan cycle is not compatible with the median voter model. The partisan cycle effect may develop if a bimodal distribution of voter preferences occurs or if voter protest abstention takes place. The partisan influence model asserts that macroeconomic policies are based on the partisan agenda of the in-party to the White House rather than the median voter's preference.

The partisan cycle predicts that stabilization policies and economic outcomes shift when the political party in control of the White House changes. The opposing macroeconomic agendas of the two parties align with the economic priorities of voters and interest groups that form the core constituencies of the political left and right.

Partisan economic pressures cause liberal administrations to choose policies that emphasize the attainment of low unemployment but with the possible side effect of rising inflation. Liberal presidencies are relatively unemployment averse. Liberal administrations support expansionary policies to reduce unemployment because of perceptions that market forces are often slow in adjusting to equilibrium.

Conservative presidencies tend to adopt policies that are relatively inflation averse but with the possible negative side effect of lower economic growth and higher unemployment. Partisan economic pressures cause conservative administrations to focus on maintaining low inflation. This creates a predictable business and financial environment for the invisible hand of competitive market forces to thrive. The political right and the classical macroeconomic view maintain that unemployment automatically adjusts to equilibrium through the self-correcting mechanism of competitive supply and demand forces in the labor and product markets.

Examination of unemployment and inflation during the period of 1961–2016 shows that the two PBC effects occurred idiosyncratically for different presidencies rather than systematically across all administrations. The economy exhibited partisan cycle characteristics of unemployment aversion for Democratic presidencies. Macroeconomic performance during most Republican incumbencies, on the other hand, seemed to show an electoral cycle pattern of declining unemployment during election years, followed by rising inflation after elections.

The business cycle data suggest that a mix of partisan and electoral effects may have transpired for most presidencies. Partisan effects may have occurred during the first half of presidencies for both Democratic and Republican terms. However, the electoral cycle effect of preelection economic stimulus may have occurred in the second half of presidential terms for most Democratic and Republican presidencies. Administrations may have pursued partisan macroeconomic goals in the first part of a term, but then shifted to macroeconomic opportunism in the latter part of a term as an attempt to increase the in-party reelection vote share.

Idiosyncratic PBC effects across presidencies should not be surprising. Many determinants affect macroeconomic policy and the business cycle. A single-cause explanation for macroeconomic policy and performance is too simplistic. Various interconnections occur between the macroeconomy and political influences on policy, including the electoral cycle, the partisan cycle, or some combination of the two PBC influences.

In addition, the president must have the power to dictate macroeconomic policy for the partisan cycle or the electoral cycle to take place. However, the president's ability to influence fiscal and monetary policies is limited. In determining macroeconomic policies, a complex and fluid dynamic occurs among the president, Congress, the Fed, and the two main political parties.

Congress and the administration are frequently in opposition in determining fiscal policy. This is especially true if partisan gridlock or a divided government occurs. Partisan gridlock on fiscal policy happens if one political party has a majority of seats in Congress while the other political party controls the presidency.

Political influences on the Fed and monetary policy can also be complex. The executive and legislative branches, as well as financial interests, can have some indirect pressure on the monetary policy actions of the central bank. Congress has oversight power on the Fed, whereas the president appoints the Fed Chairperson. In addition, many members of the FOMC and the Board of Governors have career affiliations to the finance and banking industries.

Overall, a simplifying assumption of PBC theory is that the president indirectly determines fiscal and monetary policies. Criticisms of this assumption is one of the strongest challenges against the systematic occurrence of electoral and partisan cycle effects.

Also, the impact of stabilization policies on the economy must be accurately predictable for the electoral cycle or the partisan cycle to take place. Some uncertainty exists in this regard. Forecasting economic performance can sometimes be imprecise, particularly when attempting to predict the timing of expansionary and contractionary turns in the business cycle. Some ambiguity is inevitable.

The luck and partial unpredictability of the economy is a source of risk for the reelection prospects of the in-party. The political fortune of elected officials is tied to the volatility, uncertainty, and partial uncontrollability of the economy. The incumbent faces peril of losing reelection if the economy is in a slump on election eve, even if the weak economy is unrelated to the president's policies. The incumbent stands a high chance of winning reelection if economic growth is high in an election year, even if the strong economy is unrelated to the administration's actions.

Noneconomic factors also impact presidential elections and incumbent job approval. Some noneconomic influences on the presidential vote and incumbent popularity are similar. Other effects are different. Presidential scandals, voter opinion inertia, and the presidential honeymoon influence incumbent approval. The incumbency effect and political party duration affect presidential elections. War casualties impact both presidential popularity and election outcomes.

The economy affects Congressional House and Senate elections. Economic influence on Congressional elections is similar to economic influence on presidential elections. For on-term elections, the economy impacts the outcomes through the presidential coattail. If a strong economy causes the presidential reelection vote share to be high, then this spills over and causes the in-party Congressional vote shares to also be high because of the coattail.

For midterm Congressional elections, the economy indirectly affects outcomes through the presidential approval effect. If a strong economy causes incumbent popularity to be high in a midterm year, then this spills over and may cause the in-party House and Senate vote shares to also be high in the midterm election.

One noneconomic determinant on midterm elections is the balancing effect. The balancing effect on midterm Congressional elections counters the coattail effect upon on-term Congressional elections. The presidential coattail causes an increase in votes for legislators of the party that wins the White House in on-term elections. However, House and Senate vote shares for the in-party tend to decline in midterm elections through the balancing effect. Citizens tend to vote for the out-party in midterm elections.

Besides voting behavior and presidential approval, the economy affects other measures of public opinion. Some of these indicators are consumer sentiment, the social happiness index, voter participation rates, and macropartisanship.

Political and ideological factors also impact international economic policies such as trade. The political right generally adheres to the perspective of economic liberalism. This viewpoint embraces free trade. Economic liberalism maintains that unrestricted international trade especially benefits consumers. Competitive international market forces create lower product prices, greater variety of goods, and increased product quality.

The political left sometimes adheres to the neomercantilist perspective. This outlook is protectionist on international trade. Neomercantilism supports the use of trade barriers such as tariffs and quotas to protect workers from job displacement due to imports based on international economic competition.

Another perspective on globalism and international capitalism is economic structuralism. The structuralist view maintains that international trade, international finance, and globalism tend to benefit large MNCs and rich countries. On the other hand, LDCs, low-income households, natural resources, and the environment are often exploited because of the profit incentive of capitalism.

In summary, various linkages take place in the circular flow of the political macroeconomy. Economic, ideological, and political considerations impact international trade policy, whether free trade or trade protection, and the corresponding effect on consumers, businesses, jobs, GDP, and the environment. Partisan, electoral, ideological, and special interest factors influence the decisions of the fiscal and monetary poli-cymakers. These policies affect the economy and swings in the business cycle. Macroeconomic events then influence citizen opinions and voting patterns in presidential and Congressional elections.

To be reelected, the president and Congress must consider voter opinions on the economy. The president and Congress must also take into account partisan economic platforms to maintain support from their political base. The Fed Chair may be influenced by the president, Congress, and financial interests. Various political determinants impact macroeconomic and international policies and the state of the economy. Simultaneously, the economy impacts partisan priorities, citizen attitudes, and voting. Although some general patterns appear to occur, politico-macroeconomic interactions are not fully systematic and not always predictable. Political macroeconomic interconnections take place in a fluid environment of political and economic uncertainty and idiosyncrasy.

References

Abramowitz, A. I., and J. A. Segal. 1992. *Senate Elections*. Ann Arbor, MI: University of Michigan Press.

Abrams, B. A., and P. Iossifov. 2006. "Does the Fed Contribute to a Political Business Cycle?" *Public Choice* 129, no. 3–4, pp. 249–62.

Alesina, A., and J. Sachs. 1988. "Political Parties and the Business Cycle in the United States, 1948–1984." *Journal of Money, Credit, and Banking* 20, pp. 63–82.

Balaam, D. N., and B. Dillman. 2019. *Introduction to International Political Economy*. 7th ed. New York, NY: Routledge.

Board of Governors of the Federal Reserve System (US). "M1 Money Stock [M1]," FRED, Federal Reserve Bank of St. Louis. https://fred.stlouisfed.org/series/M1, (October 28, 2019).

Campbell, J., and J. Sumners. 1990. "Presidential Coattails in Senate Elections." *The American Political Science Review* 84, no. 2, pp. 513–24.

Carbaugh, R. J. 2017. *International Economics*. 16th ed. Boston, MA: Cengage Learning.

Carlsen, F. 2000. "Unemployment, Inflation and Government Popularity—Are There Partisan Effects?" *Electoral Studies* 19, no. 2, pp. 141–50.

Chappell, H. W. 1983. "Presidential Popularity and Macroeconomic Performance: Are Voters Really So Naive?" *The Review of Economics and Statistics* 65, no. 3, pp. 385–92.

Downs, A. 1957. *An Economic Theory of Democracy*. New York, NY: Harper and Row.

Dornbusch, R., S. Fischer, and R. Startz. 2011. *Macroeconomics*, 11th ed. New York, NY: McGraw-Hill.

Fair, R. C. 1978. "The Effect of Economic Events on Votes for the President." *Review of Economics and Statistics* 60, pp. 159–73.

Fair, R. C. 2009. "Presidential and Congressional Vote-Share Equations." *American Journal of Political Science* 53, no. 1, pp. 55–72.

Federal Reserve Economic Data. FRED, Federal Reserve Bank of St. Louis. https://fred.stlouisfed.org.

Fox, G. T. 2003. "Interrelationship Between Presidential Approval, Presidential Votes and Macroeconomic Performance, 1948–2000." *Journal of Macroeconomics* 25, no. 3, pp. 411–24.

Fox, G. T. 2009. "Partisan Divide on War and the Economy: Presidential Approval of G.W. Bush." *Journal of Conflict Resolution* 53, pp. 905–33.

Fox, G. T. 2013. "War Casualties, Macroeconomic Time Inconsistency, and the Presidential Vote." In *War: Global Assessment, Public Attitudes and Psychological Effects*, ed. N. R. White, pp. 157–72. Hauppauge, NY: Nova Science Publishers, Inc.

Frey, B. S., and A. Stutzer. 2002. *Happiness and Economics: How the Economy and Institutions Affect Human Well-being*. Princeton, NJ: Princeton University Press.

Friedman, M. 1968. "The Role of Monetary Policy." *American Economic Review* 68, no. 1, pp. 1–17.

Gilpin, R. 1987. *The Political Economy of International Relations*. Princeton, NJ: Princeton University Press.

Hibbs, D. A. 1982. "On the Demand for Economic Outcomes: Macroeconomic Performance and Mass Political Support in the United States, Great Britain, and Germany." *The Journal of Politics* 44, pp. 426–62.

Hibbs, D. A. 2008. "Implications of the 'Bread and Peace' Model for the 2008 US Presidential Election." *Public Choice* 137, pp. 1–10.

Grier, K. 1989. "On the Existence of a Political Monetary Cycle." *American Journal of Political Science* 33, no. 2, pp. 376–89.

Kernell, S. 1978. "Explaining Presidential Popularity." *The American Political Science Review* 72, no. 2, pp. 506–22.

Keynes, J. M. 1936. *The General Theory of Employment, Interest, and Money*. Cambridge, UK: Macmillan Cambridge University Press.

Kydland, F. and E. Prescott. 1977. "Rules Rather Than Discretion: The Inconsistency of Optimal Policy Plans." *Journal of Political Economy* 85, pp. 473–90.

Lindbeck, A. 1976. "Stabilization Policy in Open Economies with Endogenous Politicians." *American Economic Review Papers and Proceedings* 66, pp. 1–19.

MacKuen, M. B., R. S. Erikson, and J. A. Stimson. 1989. "Macropartisanship." *American Political Science Review* 83, no. 4, pp. 1125–42.

McRae, D. 1977. "A Political Model of the Business Cycle." *Journal of Political Economy* 85, pp. 239–63.

Nordhaus, W. D. 1975. "The Political Business Cycle." *The Review of Economic Studies* 42, no. 2, pp. 169–90.

Nordhaus, W. D., A. Alesina, and C. Schultze. 1989. "Alternative Approaches to the Political Business Cycle: Comments and Discussion." *Brookings Papers on Economic Activity* 2, pp. 1–68.

Okun, Arthur, 1962. "Potential GNP: Its Measurement and Significance," *Proceedings of the Business and Economics Statistics Section*, American Statistical Association, pp. 89–104.

Porter, M. E. 1990. *Competitive Advantage of Nations*. New York, NY: The Free Press.

Phillips, A. W. 1958. "The Relation Between Unemployment and the Rate of Change of Money Wage Rates in the United Kingdom, 1861–1957." *Economica* 25, no. 100, pp. 283–99.

Rogoff, K. 1990. "Equilibrium Political Budget Cycles." *American Economic Review* 80, pp. 21–36.

Shi, M., and J. Svensson. 2006. "Political Budget Cycles: Do They Differ Across Countries and Why?" *Journal of Public Economics* 90, pp. 1367–89.

Smyth, D. J., and P. Dua. 1989. "The Public's Indifference Map Between Inflation and Unemployment: Empirical Evidence for the Nixon, Ford, Carter, and Reagan Presidencies." *Public Choice* 60, no. 1, pp. 71–85.

Smyth, D. J., S. W. Taylor, and P. Dua. 1999. "Estimating the Public's Social Preference Function Between Inflation and Unemployment Using Survey Data: The Survey Research Center Versus Gallup." *Empirical Economics* 24, pp. 361–72.

Swank, O. H. 1990. "Presidential Popularity and Reputation." *De Economist* 138, no. 2, pp. 168–80.

Swank, O. H. 1995. "Rational Voters in a Partisanship Model." *Social Choice and Welfare* 12, pp. 13–27.

Tufte, E. R. 1978. *Political Control of the Economy*. 2nd ed. Princeton, NJ: Princeton UP.

U.S. Bureau of Labor Statistics. FRED, Federal Reserve Bank of St. Louis. https://fred.stlouisfed.org.

U.S. Bureau of Labor Statistics. "Unemployment Rate [UNRATE]," FRED, Federal Reserve Bank of St. Louis. https://fred.stlouisfed.org/series/UNRATE, (October 28, 2019).

About the Author

Gerald T. Fox received his PhD in economics from the University of Utah. He completed his undergraduate degree in economics at Brigham Young University. Professor Fox teaches economics at High Point University. His research interests include political macroeconomics, regional economic analysis, and globalism. He has published research in the *Journal of Conflict Resolution, Applied Research in Economic Development*, and the *Journal of Macroeconomics*. He has also coauthored a major economic impact study on the furniture industry in North Carolina. He has presented research at numerous academic conferences. Dr. Fox speaks Japanese and travels to Japan in the summers. He has worked in the Philippines, Japan, Poland, France, and England. He was a visiting professor at the University of Warsaw in Poland. He has also served as Faculty-in-Residence at the University of Winchester in Winchester, UK.

Index

OTHER TITLES FROM THE ECONOMICS AND PUBLIC POLICY COLLECTION

Philip Romero, The University of Oregon and
Jeffrey Edwards, North Carolina A&T State University, *Editors*

- *A Primer on Macroeconomics, Second Edition, Volume II: Policies and Perspectives* by Thomas M. Beveridge
- *A Primer on Macroeconomics, Second Edition, Volume I: Elements and Principles* by Thomas M. Beveridge
- *Macroeconomics, Second Edition, Volume I* by David G. Tuerck
- *Macroeconomics, Second Edition, Volume II* by David G. Tuerck
- *Economic Renaissance In the Age of Artificial Intelligence* by Apek Mulay
- *Disaster Risk Management: Case Studies in South Asian Countries* by Huong Ha, R. Lalitha S. Fernando, and Sanjeev Kumar Mahajan
- *The Option Strategy Desk Reference: An Essential Reference for Option Traders* by Russell A. Stultz
- *Disaster Risk Management in Agriculture: Case Studies in South Asian Countries* by Huong Ha, Lalitha S. Fernando and Sanjeev Kumar Mahajan
- *Understanding Demonetization in India: A Deft Stroke of Economic Policy* by Shrawan Kumar Singh
- *Urban Development 2120* by Peter Nelson
- *Foreign Direct Investment: The Indian Experience* by Leena Ajit Kaushal
- *A Guide to International Economics* by Shahruz Mohtadi
- *The Options Trading Primer: Using Rules-Based Option Trades to Earn a Steady Income* by Russell A. Stultz

Announcing the Business Expert Press Digital Library

Concise e-books business students need for classroom and research

This book can also be purchased in an e-book collection by your library as

- *a one-time purchase,*
- *that is owned forever,*
- *allows for simultaneous readers,*
- *has no restrictions on printing, and*
- *can be downloaded as PDFs from within the library community.*

Our digital library collections are a great solution to beat the rising cost of textbooks. E-books can be loaded into their course management systems or onto students' e-book readers. The **Business Expert Press** digital libraries are very affordable, with no obligation to buy in future years. For more information, please visit **www.businessexpertpress.com/librarians**. To set up a trial in the United States, please email **sales@businessexpertpress.com**.

www.ingramcontent.com/pod-product-compliance
Lightning Source LLC
Chambersburg PA
CBHW061218220326
41599CB00025B/4675